Currency Options
for Retail Traders

Dana DeCecco
Former Commodity Trading Advisor and 15
year independent trader.

Dana has authored hundreds of published financial articles. His
first book, "2 Trade Smart", covers the basic methods of technical
analysis. He maintains four websites dedicated to basic and
advanced trading skills.

Lakeside21.com

DISCLAIMER
   Trading futures, forex, stocks, and options involves the risk of loss. Please consider carefully whether futures, forex, stocks, or options are appropriate to your financial situation. Only risk capital should be used when trading. Investors could lose more than their original investment. You must review the customer account agreement prior to establishing an account. Past results are not indicative of future results. The risk of loss in trading can be substantial, carefully consider the inherent risks of such an investment in light of your financial condition. The author is not affiliated with any brokers, people, or companies mentioned. Opinions expressed by the author are by no means a solicitation of any kind.

Before trading options please read the publication "Characteristics and Risks of Standardized Options" available from your options broker.

DEDICATION

This book is dedicated to my Princess, Cheyanna.
A gifted and talented young lady.

CONTENTS

ACKNOWLEDGMENTS

Big Dan DeCecco for his skillful photography

For charts and images:
Nasdaq OMX
Rydex Currency Shares
CME Group
Saxo Bank
Option Oracle
FreeStock Charts.com
MT4 Forex Platform
DailyFX.com
OptionsXpress
Fed. Reserve Bank of NY
ForexFactory.com
TDAmeritrade, Think-or-Swim
AVA Forex
Quick Screen Capture
Barchart.com
CBOE
OIC
Ivolatility.com
FXBridge
Ikon Global
FX360.com

1 The Playing Field

The purpose of this book is to simplify the option trading process. Option trading can be complicated and time consuming but it does not have to be. I have developed analysis techniques that are simple and easy to use. This book will show you how I trade options. The reader should have some prior understanding of option trading.

Currency options provide trading opportunities that are not available in most other asset classes. The Foreign Exchange market is by far the largest market in the world. Options on currency pairs and indexes have recently become available to the retail trader.

Controlled risk trading is possible due to the availability of currency options previously only available to banks and institutional investors. It is possible to develop trades with very little risk and unlimited profit potential. The Black & Scholes option pricing model, originally created for the stock market, underestimates the probability of strong directional spot movements.

Option prices are skewed toward the markets anticipation of directional movement. This could be considered a leading indicator for the spot forex trader. Option analysis can provide the spot forex trader an advantage in the market place.

Due to the volatile nature of the forex market, the pricing models fall short on predicting the range of movement. Non-directional trading provides an opportunity to take advantage of forex price action while mitigating the risk of a spot position.

Delta neutral trading combined with volatility assessment and our fundamental / technical market analysis can provide us a trading advantage. Various strategies of long / short spot positions combined with long / short option positions will yield low risk trades with high profit potential.

Trading implied volatility in the options market can be as profitable as trading price action. Market timing tactics can take advantage of anticipated increased volatility. An increase in implied volatility will increase the value of a purchased option.

High probability, low risk trades can be developed by using various combinations of spot and option positions. Currency options are available in the forex, futures, and equity markets.

The equities market provides currency Exchange Traded Funds (ETFs), options on these funds, and option only ETFs. The forex market offers Over The Counter (OTC) options on forex pairs. The futures market offers contracts on currencies and options on these contracts.

This wide variety of trading instruments make currency options available to all traders. Even traders with relatively small accounts can enter the currency option market. Very small accounts may have a problem overcoming broker fees and the bid / ask spread.

The profit on a one contract trade can be consumed by these factors. I suggest trading a minimum of three to five option contracts. Inverse trading greatly lowers the risk of losing your investment capital. An underfunded account can lead to failure in the trading business.

Rydex Currency Shares are available in the spot market price convention. This means you can trade spot and options on these equity products.

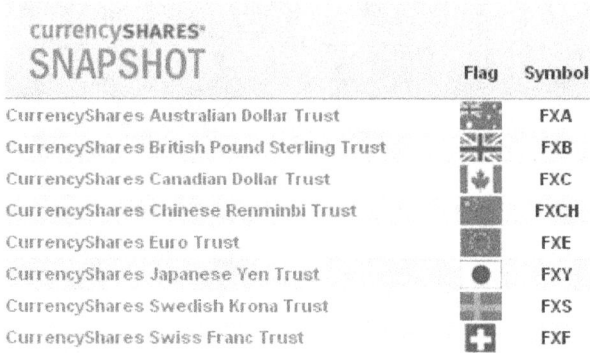

currencySHARES® SNAPSHOT	Flag	Symbol
CurrencyShares Australian Dollar Trust		FXA
CurrencyShares British Pound Sterling Trust		FXB
CurrencyShares Canadian Dollar Trust		FXC
CurrencyShares Chinese Renminbi Trust		FXCH
CurrencyShares Euro Trust		FXE
CurrencyShares Japanese Yen Trust		FXY
CurrencyShares Swedish Krona Trust		FXS
CurrencyShares Swiss Franc Trust		FXF

Nasdaq OMX offers PHLX World Currency Options. These equity products can only be traded using options.

Easy-to-use with standardized underlying contracts:

10,000 UNITS	SYMBOL	
AUSTRALIAN DOLLAR	XDA	
BRITISH POUND	XDB	
CANADIAN DOLLAR	XDC	
EURO	XDE	
SWISS FRANC	XDS	
NEW ZEALAND DOLLAR	XDZ	
1,000,000 UNITS	SYMBOL	
JAPANESE YEN	XDN	

The International Securities Exchange (ISE) offers Fxoptions on currency pairs. There is little volume or open interest on these products. I would avoid them.

CURRENCY	per US $	SYMBOL	in US $	SYMBOL
Australian dollar	USD/AUD	AUX	AUD/USD	AUM
Brazilian real	USD/BRL	BRB	BRL/USD	-
British pound	USD/GBP	BPX	GBP/USD	GBP
Canadian dollar	USD/CAD	CDD	CAD/USD	-
Euro	USD/EUR	EUI	EUR/USD	EUU
Japanese yen	USD/JPY	YUK	JPY/USD	-
Mexican peso	USD/MXN	PZO	MXN/USD	-
New Zealand dollar	USD/NZD	NZD	NZD/USD	NDO
Swedish krona	USD/SEK	SKA	SEK/USD	-
Swiss franc	USD/CHF	SFC	CHF/USD	-

There are many more equity products available and more coming soon. The popularity of forex trading has attracted new participants in the market place. Everyone wants a piece of the pie.

Some of the equity products are heavily traded but many are not. This situation creates a liquidity problem. Since the Option Clearing Corporation is obliged to settle all option contracts, getting paid is not a problem. The problem lies in the spread. If the bid and ask prices are too wide the contract is not tradable. I will cover this in a later chapter.

Due to the liquidity problem in the equity market, I prefer trading the Futures market or the OTC market (not available to retail traders in the USA). The futures market is a mystery to many traders but this book will explain and simplify this market to the extent that it can be simplified.

The equities market can still provide some excellent trading opportunities and is well suited to traders with a small trading account. A trader with a $5,000 account can do quite well in the equities market. A trading account size of $2,000 is cutting it close.

The Chicago Merchantile Exchange, or CME Group, offers a wide variety of FX futures products. I am providing an exhaustive list of products in order for this book to be a reference manual for the currency options trader.

G10 Currency Pairs (CME)

AUD/USD	FUT | OPT
AUD/CAD	FUT
AUD/JPY	FUT
AUD/NZD	FUT
CAD/USD	FUT | OPT
CAD/JPY	FUT
CHF/USD	FUT | OPT
CHF/JPY	FUT
Dow Jones CME FX$INDEX	FUT
EUR/USD	FUT | OPT
E-mini EUR/USD	FUT
EUR/AUD	FUT
EUR/GBP	FUT | OPT
EUR/CAD	FUT
EUR/CHF	FUT | OPT
EUR/JPY	FUT | OPT
EUR/NOK	FUT
EUR/SEK	FUT

G10 Currency Pairs (cont.)

GBP/USD	FUT | OPT
GBP/JPY	FUT
GBP/CHF	FUT
JPY/USD	FUT | OPT
E-mini JPY/USD	FUT
NOK/USD	FUT
NZD/USD	FUT | OPT
SEK/USD	FUT

E-micros (CME)

E-micro AUD/USD	FUT
E-micro EUR/USD	FUT
E-micro GBP/USD	FUT
E-micro CAD/USD	FUT
E-micro USD/CAD	FUT
E-micro CHF/USD	FUT
E-micro USD/CHF	FUT
E-micro JPY/USD	FUT
E-micro USD/JPY	FUT
E-micro USD/RMB	FUT

Emerging Market Currency Pairs (CME)

▪ BRL/USD	FUT | OPT
▪ CZK/USD	FUT | OPT
▪ CZK/EUR	FUT | OPT
▪ HUF/EUR	FUT | OPT
▪ HUF/USD	FUT | OPT
▪ ILS/USD	FUT | OPT
▪ KRW/USD	FUT | OPT
▪ MXN/USD	FUT | OPT
▪ PLN/USD	FUT | OPT
▪ PLN/EUR	FUT | OPT
▪ RMB/USD	FUT | OPT
▪ RMB/EUR	FUT | OPT
▪ RMB/JPY	FUT | OPT
▪ RUB/USD	FUT | OPT
▪ ZAR/USD	FUT | OPT
▪ USD/RMB	FUT
▪ USD/TRY	FUT
▪ EUR/TRY	FUT

FX VolContracts (CME)

▪ EUR/USD 1-month Realized Volatility futures	FUT
▪ EUR/USD 3-month Realized Volatility futures	FUT

As you can see there are more products than anyone would care to trade. The best trading strategy is to become very familiar with a handful of assets and learn how they move and react to different market conditions. Most of the examples in this book will use the EUR/USD pair. This is the most heavily traded currency pair.

Futures contracts are derivatives. Options contracts on futures contracts are actually derivatives on derivatives which can get quite confusing. The average retail trader is not interested in taking possession of a foreign currency. We are simply trying to profit from the anticipated future market conditions.

There is no way I can teach you everything about the futures and options markets in this tiny book. But I can show you everything you need to know to trade these markets profitably. Further educational sources are prolific on the internet from an abundance of sources including your broker.

I would suggest using this book as a primer to get you up and running. The market is always changing with new FX products on the way. Nasdaq OMX is currently developing new currency products. You need to stay informed and further education is well advised.

The OTC (Over The COUNTER) FX option market is available to retail traders living outside the USA. These FX products are not exchange traded and the counter-party to your trade is responsible for contract fulfillment. There is no liquidity problem if you are trading near the money options.

Here is a chart of the most liquid contracts available from Saxo Bank with Implied Volatility.

Pair	Spot	1w	1m	3m	6m	1y
EURUSD	1.4372 (0.69%)	9.3 (-0.2)	9.6 (+0.1)	10.6 (-0.15)	11.5 (-0.05)	12.3 (-0.05)
USDJPY	82.91 (0.66%)	9.8 (-0.7)	10.65 (+0)	11.55 (-0.3)	12.65 (-0.1)	13.78 (-0.17)
GBPUSD	1.6283 (0.26%)	7.5 (-0.6)	8.05 (-0.2)	8.95 (-0.1)	9.85 (-0.2)	10.75 (-0.2)
AUDUSD	1.0568 (-0.45%)	9.7 (-0.4)	10.7 (-0.1)	12.15 (-0.1)	13.05 (+0)	13.85 (+0)
USDCAD	0.9622 (-0.04%)	7.7 (-0.5)	7.9 (-0.3)	8.6 (+0)	9.3 (+0)	9.8 (+0)
USDCHF	0.8943 (-0.05%)	9.65 (-0.8)	9.9 (-0.1)	10.65 (-0.12)	11.15 (-0.03)	11.55 (-0.1)
EURJPY	119.16 (1.34%)	13.65 (-0.6)	13.95 (-0.5)	14.35 (+0.1)	14.6 (+0)	15.4 (+0.1)
EURGBP	0.8826 (0.44%)	7.9 (-0.1)	7.95 (-0.2)	8.85 (-0.1)	9.45 (-0.1)	10.05 (+0.05)
EURCHF	1.2851 (0.63%)	9.3 (-0.2)	9.35 (+0.1)	9.95 (+0.1)	10.2 (+0.05)	10.3 (+0.05)
GOLD	1486.36 (-0.77%)	11.75 (+0)	12.5 (-0.1)	14.2 (-0.1)	16.2 (+0)	19.1 (+0)
SILVER	43.2122 (-2.36%)	32.5 (+1.5)	32.6 (+0.2)	34 (+0.4)	34.05 (-0.3)	34.35 (-0.2)

The list of all OTC options is quite long. Although OTC products are not exchange traded and guaranteed by the OCC, I don't see any OTC traders complaining. The platforms are easy to learn and spot / option positions can be easily traded on the same platform.

The above chart indicates that volatility is low on a number of pairs and gold. This is a good time to buy options. Volatility is a major factor in the pricing of options. Option information sources can be used from one market to trade another. If volatility is low in the OTC market, it is also low in the equity market and the futures market.

There are volumes of books written about option trading. Many online resources are available covering every conceivable aspect of option trading except for much of the information contained in this book. My trading approach is unique, simple, and effective. My target is high probability, low risk trades.

Since most options expire worthless it would stand to reason that most option traders lose money. I think that many option traders approach the market as a gambling venture. The goal of trading options should be a controlled risk, short term investment strategy.

Options are basically short term contracts on an underlying asset. They are normally traded with a directional bias of the underlying asset in mind. For example, If you expect the price of XYZ company to rise, you would buy a call option. If you expect the price to fall, you would buy a put option.

Options can also be traded without a directional bias in mind. If the market makes a substantial move in any direction the trade will be profitable. On the other side of the coin, profitable trades can be set up with little or no price movement of the underlying asset due to the factor of implied volatility.

I have covered much of our FX option playing field. Binary and Box options are also forms of currency option trading but do not apply to the trading systems in this book. They are both valid forms of option trading with interesting possibilities.

Before researching an options trade, analysis of the underlying asset is essential. My preferred form of analysis is technical analysis or chart reading. To become adept at reading price charts please refer to my first book "2 Trade Smart", available from Amazon books.

2 Non-Linear Trading

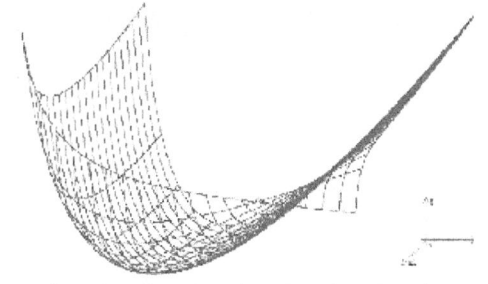

Option trading and option pricing are both non-linear. The trading and pricing of options is not an exact science. Flaws in option pricing create trading opportunities providing us an edge.

I am not a scientist or a mathematician, but I do have common sense. When options became available on forex products, I studied the chains. I anticipated finding flaws because of the volatile nature of forex and the existing pricing models that were created for the stock market.

The exchanges are aware of these discrepancies but have been unable to come up with a solution. Most retail traders are not aware of it. Watch the spread. They can widen the spread to compensate for the premium.

A great deal of research has been done on this subject by people that are way smarter than me. You can find published reports at:
http://www.hub.sciverse.com/action/search/results?st=non-linear+options+pricing

So what exactly are linear and non-linear trades ?

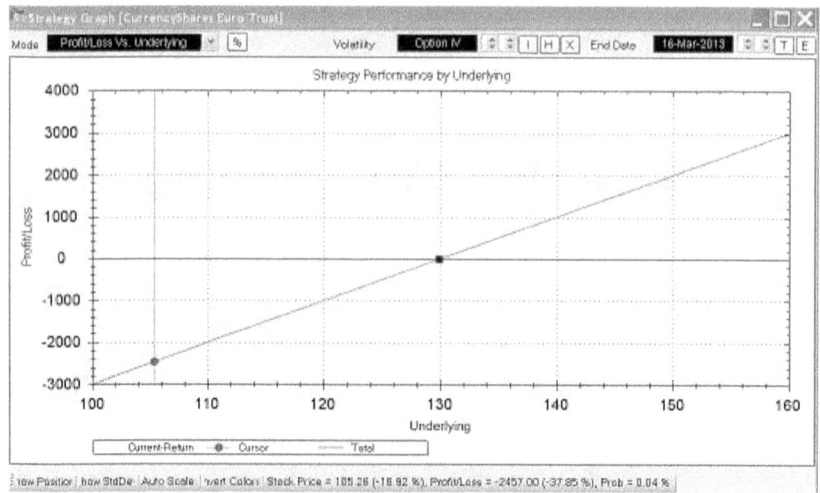

This is a graph of a linear trade made with the free OptionsOracle platform available from Samoa Sky. The underlying asset is FXE (Rydex Currency Shares). In forex language it is EUR/USD and this facsimile chart can be used to research forex, futures, and equities.

The linear trade is one long position of this asset. It is a straight line trade. For each unit (or Dollar) the price increases or decreases your profit or loss will do the same.

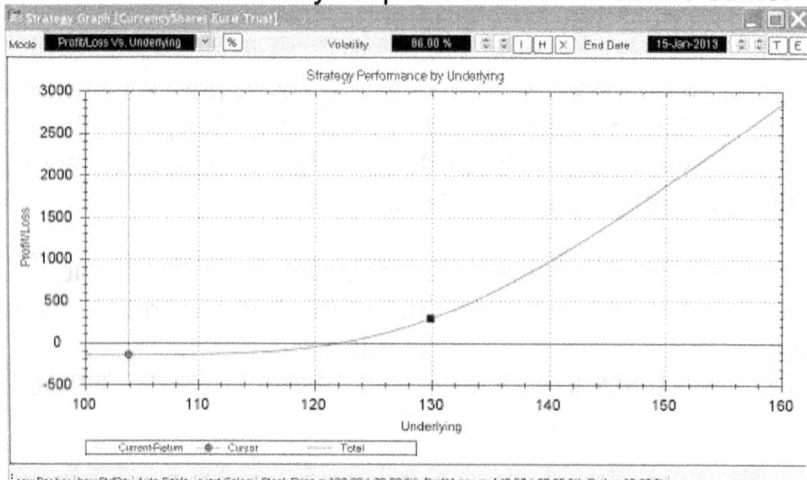

The second graph is a non-linear trade. It is one long call option contract on FXE. It is a curved line graph. For each one unit price increase in the underlying asset our trade profit increases exponentially. For each one unit decrease in the underlying asset our loss decreases exponentially. You can only lose what you paid for the option but the profit is unlimited.

The advantage to non linear trading is to cut losses and let profits run. The disadvantage is the time limit imposed by option expiration. This disadvantage can be partially overcome through the use of technical and fundamental analysis.

You should have some knowledge of option trading before reading this book but I will cover some basic terminology to make sure we are on the same page.

A few terms you should already know:

The SPOT price is the actual price of the asset.

ATM "at the money" is an option strike price very close to the actual spot price.

ITM "in the money" for a CALL the spot price is above the strike price. For a Put the spot price is below the strike price.

OTM "out of the money" (reverse of above)

ITM options are more expensive than OTM options because the Intrinsic value is greater. Intrinsic value is the actual moneyness or real value of the option. Extrinsic value is time value.

Intrinsic value moves with the price of the asset. Extrinsic value erodes with time. Option trading is a game of timing. We can time our trades using technical analysis and option chains.

There are only four basic option trades. All other complex trades are composed of a combination of these four trades.

CALLS	PUTS
• When you BUY a call you are OPENING A LONG POSITION • You are bullish on the spot movement • Maximum loss is the premium paid • Maximum profit is unlimited • To close this position you must sell the call that you purchased • When you SELL a call you are OPENING A SHORT POSITION • You are bearish on spot price movement • Maximum profit is the premium you were paid • Maximum loss is unlimited • To close this position you must buy back the call you sold	• When you BUY a put you are OPENING A SHORT POSITION • You are bearish on the spot price movement • Maximum loss is the premium paid • Maximum profit is unlimited • To close this position you must sell the put you purchased • When you SELL a put you are OPENING A LONG POSITION • You are bullish on spot price movement • Maximum gain is the premium you were paid • Maximum loss is unlimited • To close this position you must buy back the put you sold

Buying calls and puts transfer rights to the buyer such as the right to buy or sell an asset at a certain strike price. Selling (or writing) calls and puts transfer obligations to the seller. You are obligated to the buyer under the terms of the contract.

Most of the trades discussed in this book will deal with buying options. Selling options can be quite lucrative but buying is much safer. The object of this book is finding and trading high probability, low risk trades. Buying options limits your risk to the premium paid for the option and requires much less margin capital than selling options.

Currency options can be European style or American style. The premium paid for European style is less expensive because they can only be exercised at expiration. This is not a factor in our trades since we do not exercise options. We buy or sell them back before expiration or they expire worthless.

Option expiration example of EUR/USD:

Call Option assignment:

> 1.If the spot market is above the strike price at maturity, the option will be exercised and investor will have a buy position of Euro against USD .

> 2.If the spot market be at or below the strike price at expiration the option will expire worthless.

Put option assignment:

> 1.If the spot market is below the strike price the option will be exercised and investor will have a short position of Euro against USD .

> 2.If the spot market be at or above the strike price the option will expire worthless

The above example is an OTC European style contract showing the assignment at expiration. Most of the contracts we are trading are cash settled but check with your broker to make sure you don't end up with a pocketful of Yen.

We will be closing our positions before expiration. If the trade is a losing trade we will let the contract expire worthless. European style is a better choice because the premiums are cheaper. That is enough said about this subject since it should have little impact on our trading.

Understanding linear trading should be simple. If you buy XYZ stock, and it goes up one dollar, you make one dollar. Non-linear trading is a bit more complex. If you buy a call option on XYZ stock, and it goes up one dollar, your profit may go up more than one dollar. And if XYZ goes down one dollar, your profit may go down less than one dollar.

Spreads, commissions, and DELTA must be considered.

3 Delta Neutral

Delta is the ratio of the value of the option compared to the value of the asset. The delta of an ATM call should be very close to +.50. This means that if the asset price increases by one dollar the option value will increase by fifty cents.

The delta of an ATM put should be very close to -.50. This means that for each dollar the asset decreases in value, your put option will increase in value by fifty cents. The opposite is true for an adverse price movement.

Since DELTA is one of the GREEKS in option trading, I will discuss my view of the Greeks and double cover this subject. It is the most important aspect of option trading.

DELTA is of utmost importance in my option trading. An ATM call option may have a delta of +.5 which means for each $1 the price of the asset increases, the value of the option will increase by fifty cents. An ATM put option may have a delta of -.5 which means for each $1 the price of the asset decreases, the value of the option increases fifty cents.

GAMMA is the reason delta neutral trading works. Gamma is the rate of change of delta. Gamma is greatest at or near the money and is lesser deep in or out of the money. It is this increase or decrease in delta that make delta neutral trading work.

THETA is the rate of change of the value of an option due to time decay. This tells you how much money you will lose (if buying) or make (if selling) each day due to time decay.

VEGA is sensitivity to volatility. Very, very important. I have an entire chapter on this subject.

RHO is rate of change due to interest rates. It is a factor in option pricing.

When I am setting up a trade , DELTA is pretty much the only Greek I am interested in. I don't need the other values because I always GRAPH my trade, and count up or down the chain ladder. I also do a quick VOLATILITY study. That's all I need (along with my technical analysis) to make a trade. I'm in the TMI camp. TOO MUCH INFORMATION ! There is a lot to be said for keeping it simple.

Once you grasp the fundamental concepts of option trading, the other information can be added if necessary. Complex trades can be developed and simple trades will become second nature.

The following graph illustrates the profit on a linear long position.

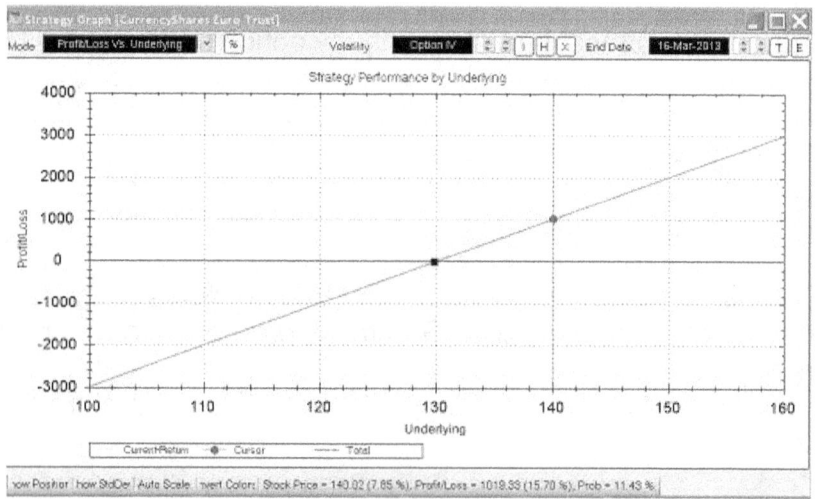

If the price of the underlying asset reaches 140, the profit will be $1000. A spot trade is a delta 1 trade.

To create a delta 1 long option trade we need to find 2 ATM option contracts that are very close to delta +.50. Two of these contracts would be very close to the delta one spot trade.

The following chart is of two delta +.49 call options. Delta .49 is as close as I could find to delta .50, and it is close enough. Now both of these trades are delta 1 trades.

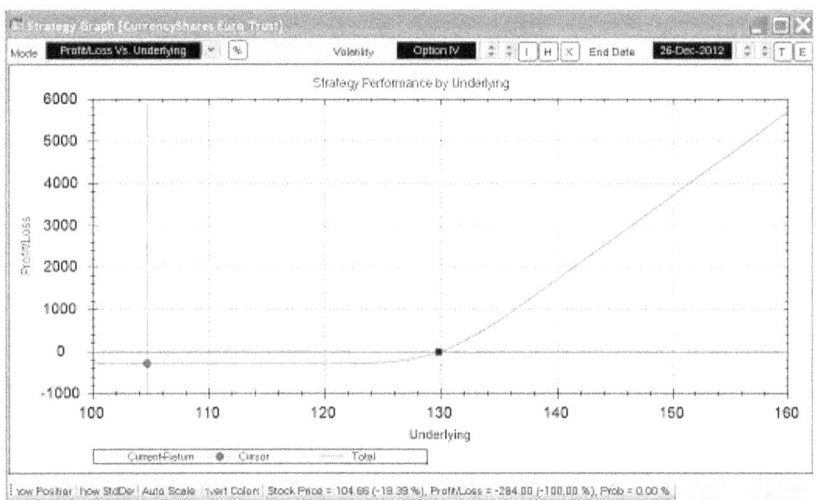

In this example of the FXE exchange traded fund if the price of the underlying reaches 140, the profit on the trade is $1721. The cost of the option, the spread and broker fees would be close to $300 leaving at least a $400 advantage for the option trade. These are the same trades with vastly different outcomes.

Can you see the advantage of the option trade? Not only is the profit greater but the risk of loss is limited to $284. The loss on the spot trade is unlimited. The disadvantage of the option trade is the time limit imposed by the contract. Market timing is the key.

To become a good option trader you must be a good spot trader to get the timing right. Basic technical analysis skills are not hard to learn.

The effect of Gamma can continue to work on the option

trade. The further the spot gets in the money the higher the delta becomes. You can get very close to a two dollar return for each one dollar movement.

The opposite is true for a losing trade. The further out of the money the spot gets, the delta decreases less and less. So you are losing less money. Does this sound like fun yet?

This illustrates the nature of a non-linear trade. You can make more and lose less than a conventional spot trade. Gamma keeps on working. In the graphs above, if the spot price reaches 150, the option trade will pay almost twice the spot trade profit.

This scenario is unlikely but illustrates a good example of the power of Gamma.

.A DELTA NEUTRAL trade is simply a trade with 2 legs where the delta totals zero.

A long ATM call (Delta +.5) and a long ATM put (Delta -.5) is a Delta Neutral trade.

Long spot (Delta +1) and long 2 ATM (Delta -1) puts is a Delta Neutral trade.

Short spot (Delta -1) and long 2 ATM (Delta +1) calls is a Delta Neutral trade.

Delta neutral trades do not work every time. You must determine if the asset you are trading will clear the break even points before the expiration date.

The delta of one long spot position is always +1. The delta of one short spot position is always -1. The delta of options is always different. ATM options are usually close to delta plus or minus .50 but you will rarely get the trade to exactly delta neutral.

Cal	129.00	19-Jan-	FXE3	2.25	0.00	0.49	2.70	2.76	112	3,043	10.04	75.82	0.763	0.09
Cal	130.00	19-Jan-	FXE3	1.79	0.00	0.73	1.95	2.00	8,238	10,753	9.60	65.19	0.663	0.11
Cal	131.00	19-Jan-	FXE3	1.35	0.00	1.05	1.29	1.32	1,268	1,481	9.00	53.29	0.541	0.13
Cal	132.00	19-Jan-	FXE3	0.77	0.00	0.82	0.80	0.82	1,325	1,332	8.76	41.19	0.403	0.13
Cal	133.00	19-Jan-	FXE3	0.48	0.00	0.48	0.46	0.48	1,186	2,352	8.67	29.95	0.274	0.11
Cal	134.00	19-Jan-	FXE3	0.25	0.00	0.26	0.24	0.26	1,516	827	8.61	20.42	0.169	0.09

In this example the ATM calls have delta's of +.541 and +.403

I would use the +.541 for the trade and consider it close enough with a slight bullish bias. Occasionally the delta will be so far off that the trade will not be feasible. In that case simply move on to the next trade.

To sum it up, the delta of an option is the amount it will pay for each spot movement of one unit. If the underlying spot price moves one dollar, a +.50 delta option will pay you fifty cents. Two +.50 delta options will pay you one dollar.

If the spot price continues to rise, the delta of the options will increase. If the option delta increases to +.75, your option position will pay you $1.50 for each one dollar increase in spot price.

This non-linear concept can greatly increase the profitability of a trade. It can also reduce the risk of loss.

4 Inverse Trading

The chart below clearly explains inverse functions. however I don't have a clue of what they are talking about. I dropped out of college and joined the Marines. If you understand this formula, then you should be teaching me. I just know how to make trades.

$$y = \frac{1}{x} - 3 \qquad \text{for } f^{-}(x)$$
$$y \cdot \frac{x}{1} = \frac{1}{y} - \frac{3 \times y}{1 \ y} \qquad \text{swap } x/y$$
$$xy = 1 - 3y \qquad y = ?$$
$$xy$$

Inverse option trades can get very complex. I am still working on an inverse bull put spread, but it goes against my rule of KEEPING IT SIMPLE.

Inverse option trades DO NOT work on most commodity ETFs. The exception to this may be gold, US Dollar index, and possibly the major indexes. I have already researched this. Don't waste your time, the Market Makers are on to you. The spreads are too wide and the payoff too low. Inverse option trades on currency futures options are an excellent opportunity. Inverse option trades using OTC options are easy and fast to get in and out. I would stay ATM on major pairs for liquidity sake when trading OTC options.

I normally trade the major currency pairs: EURUSD, GBPUSD, AUDUSD, USDJPY, USDCAD, USDCHF unless I spot a good opportunity. The major pairs are more liquid and the bid / ask spread is tighter.

Lets examine an inverse option trade on FXE which is EUR/USD. The chart below shows the upper and lower break even prices and the maximum loss. This trade is a delta neutral long call and long put.

Strategy Summary

Criteria	Price	Change	Prob	Total	Total %	Total
Total Investment				230.00		
Total Debit				230.00		
Maximum Profit Poten...	Infinity	Infinity		Infinity		
Maximum Loss Risk	130.00	0.13 %	49.12...	-230.00	-100.0	-33.89 %
Lower Breakeven	127.70	-1.64 %	38.97...	0.00		
Upper Breakeven	132.30	1.90 %	37.48...	0.00		
Total Theta [day]				-4.75	-2.07 %	

The total investment is $230 per contract so the maximum loss is $230 per contract traded. This loss is only possible if FXE stays at the same exact price until contract expiration.

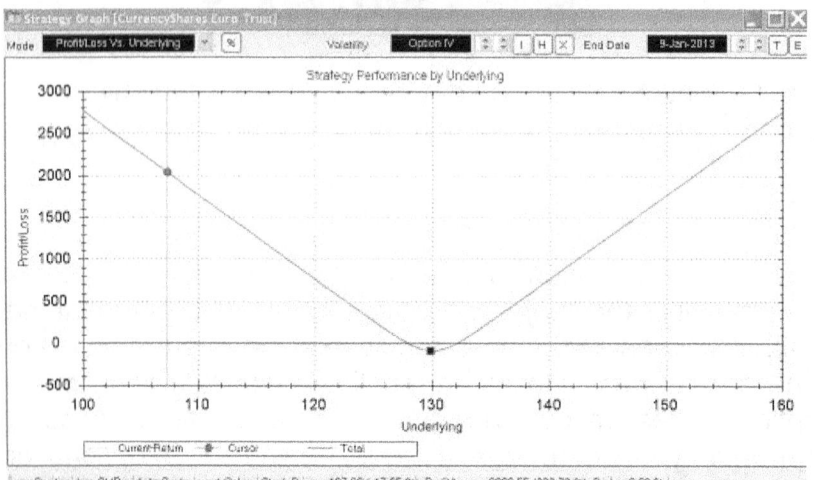

If FXE moves in either direction it improves the status of the trade. The currency market is prone to large directional movements. Once past the break even prices, the trade will become profitable.

Lets examine a delta neutral trade on XAU which is the PHLX gold and silver index. This trade is one long call contract and one long put contract.

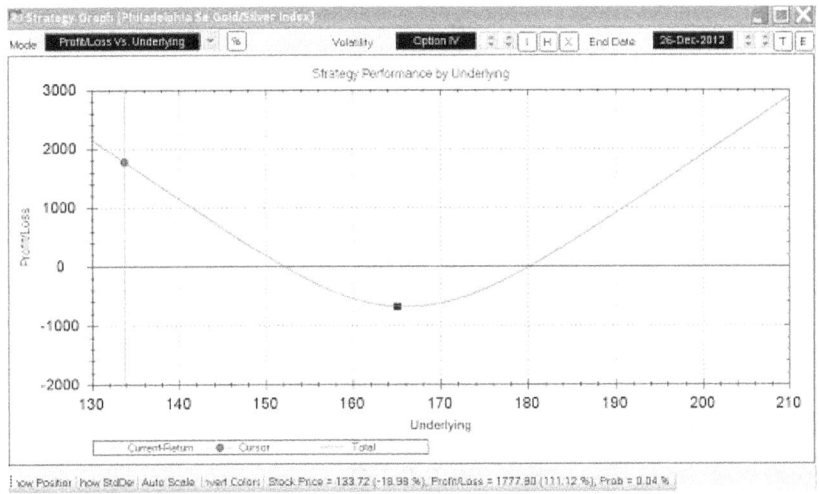

This chart is not what we're looking for. The break even points are too wide. The underlying asset will never cover this much ground before expiration. No trade here.

Next is a delta neutral option trade on SPY, Spiders Trust follows the SP-500 and is heavily traded. The same long call and long put will be used.

Strategy Summary

Criteria	Price	Change	Prob	Total	Total %	Total
Total Investment				280.00		
Total Debit				280.00		
Maximum Profit Poten...	Infinity	Infinity		Infinity		
Maximum Loss Risk	142.00	-0.25 %	46.76...	-280.00	-100.0	-175.94
Lower Breakeven	139.20	-2.21 %	23.02...	0.00		
Upper Breakeven	145.80	2.42 %	21.48...	0.00		
Total Theta [day]				-19.24	-6.87 %	

The investment is $280 per contract and the maximum loss is the $280 paid plus broker fees (I am not including broker fees in the calculations because they can vary widely.

23

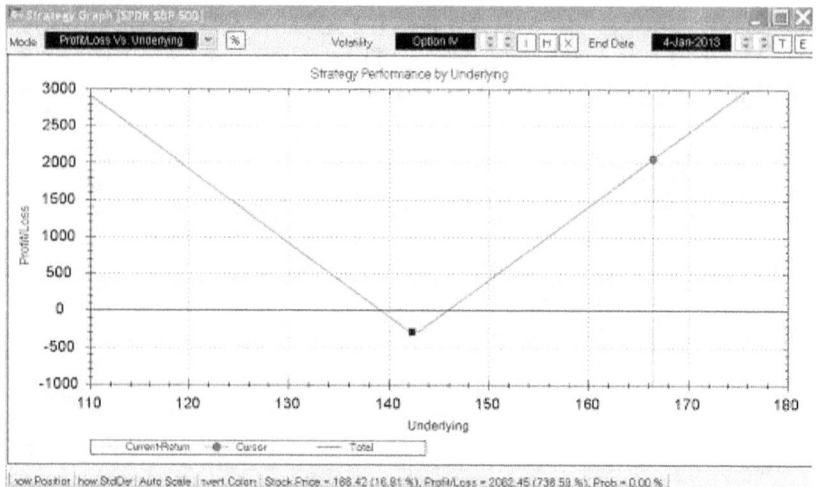

This is a much better picture than we saw with XAU.

We can check out the actual price chart to determine if the price will pass the break even points.

The horizontal lines are the break even points from our trade. I think the price could go beyond the break even lines within the 30 days of our contract expiration. We will determine at what point we will exit the trade before entering the trade. Please refer to my first book "2 Trade Smart" to learn how to trade these markets. Option trading is no different than spot trading when it comes to entry and exit points.

This particular trade is a possibility and I will put it on the shelf while I search for a better opportunity.

The next set of graphics is an inverse option trade on FXB which is GBP/USD. A delta neutral call and put.

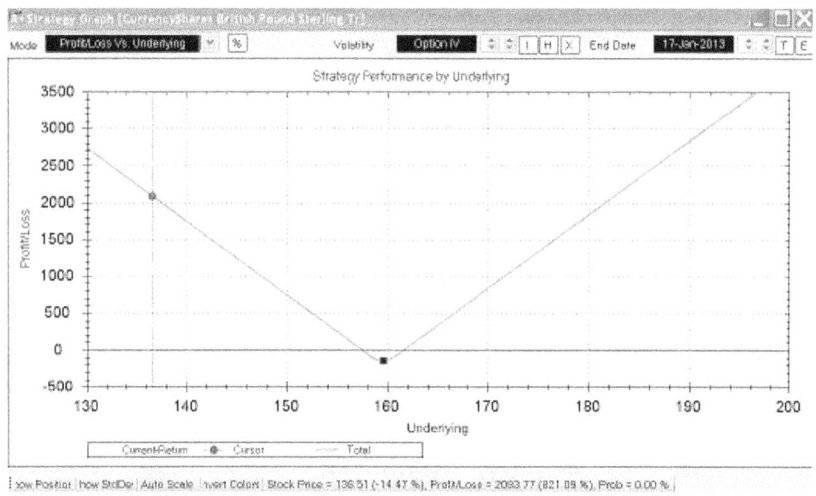

At first glance, this graph looks good.

Strategy Summary

Criteria	Price	Change	Prob	Total	Total %	Total
Total Investment				255.00		
Total Debit				255.00		
Maximum Profit Poten...	Infinity	Infinity		Infinity		
Maximum Loss Risk	159.00	-0.38 %	41.30...	-155.00	-60.78 %	-55.28 %
Lower Breakeven	157.45	-1.35 %	21.42...	0.00		
Upper Breakeven	161.55	1.22 %	23.92...	0.00		
Total Theta [day]				-3.62	-1.42 %	

The total investment is $255 per contract traded. The upper and lower break even seems to be reasonable, but lets examine the price chart to see if we have a trade here.

The GBP/USD price chart below will tell the tale.

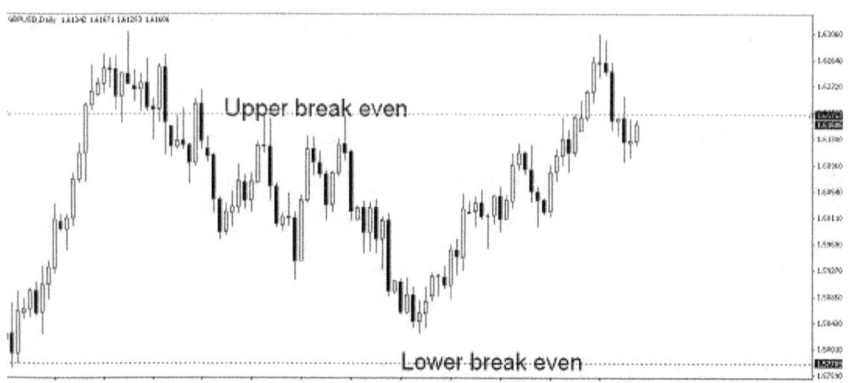

The upper break even line is great but the lower break even line is way out of line. There is no trade here but this chart may give us a clue as to market sentiment.

Since the upper break even line is so close and the lower line is very far away, the options market must have expectations of a declining price. The market is generally set up so that the greatest number of participants will lose money. That is why most options expire worthless.

The break even lines must be a reasonable distance from the actual price. The chart above is the daily time frame. There is no way the price can exceed the lower break even before option expiration. I spent less than three minutes researching this trade. Do your homework.

Take your time and only enter the best trades. Allow enough time for the price to move before expiration. The FXE trade is the best we have seen so far. EUR/USD is the most heavily traded pair. The bid/ask spread is normally tight and the daily ATR (Average True Range) is relatively high.

Forex pairs have different daily, weekly, and monthly average ranges. Knowing how far the price normally travels will help us select which pairs to trade.

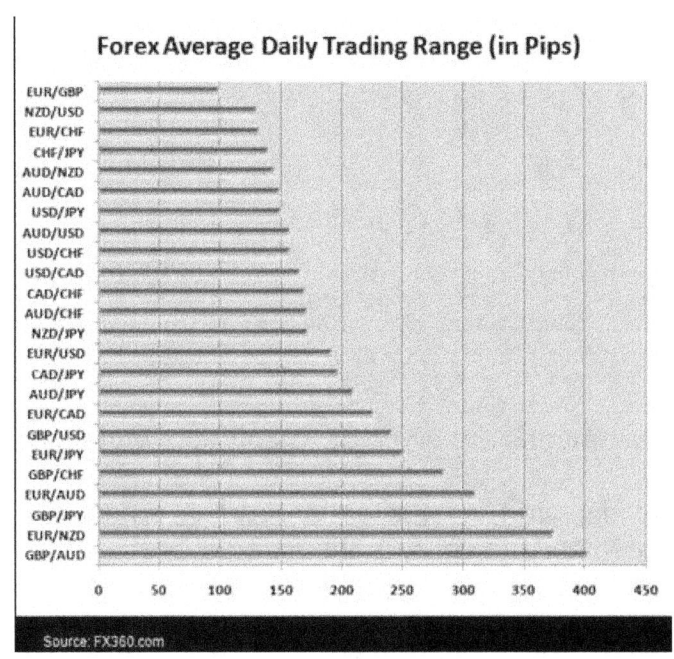

The above range chart was created by FX360.com. It will give you an idea of which pairs are most volatile.

OptionsXpress provides option analysis tools and excellent charting.

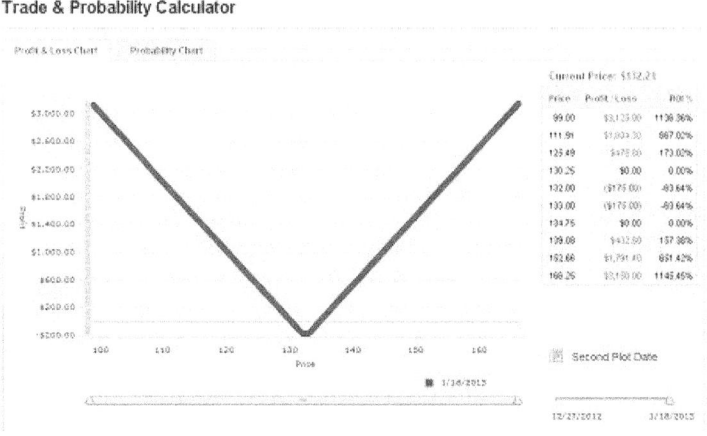

The above images are of the optionsXpress trade calculator.

We have explored inverse option trading. There is another type of inverse trading. It is the inverse spot / option trade. You trade the spot in one direction and the option in another.

The inverse spot / option trade uses the LINEAR nature of the spot trade and the NON LINEAR nature of the options trade. It works due to the VOLATILE nature of the forex market.

Long spot is + 1 delta
Long 2 ATM put contracts is -1 delta
If you make both legs of this trade you are Delta Neutral

Scenario 1: Your spot trade increases in value at the rate of delta 1 ($1 per pip). Your option trade decreases in value in a non linear fashion. When this trade is near the money the option will decrease in value $1 as the spot increases $1. Due to GAMMA, once it begins to move out of the money, your option may be losing only $.70 for each dollar gained by spot, and soon only $.50.

Your spot trade continues to increase at the rate of $1 per pip. Your option continues to retain value because you are not losing $1 for each 1 pip spot movement. The result is that you will gain more on the spot trade than you will lose on the option trade. During periods of high volatility, this difference can be substantial.

Scenario 2: Your spot trade decreases in value at the rate of delta 1 ($1 per pip). Your option trade increases in value in a non linear fashion. When this trade is near the money the option will increase in value $1 as the spot decreases $1. Due to GAMMA, once it begins to move in the money, your option may be gaining $1.30 for each dollar lost by spot, and soon $1.50.

Your spot continues to to decrease in value at the rate of $1 per pip. Your options delta continues to increase to the point where it could have a delta of +2. At that point, your option is making $2 for each dollar lost by spot.

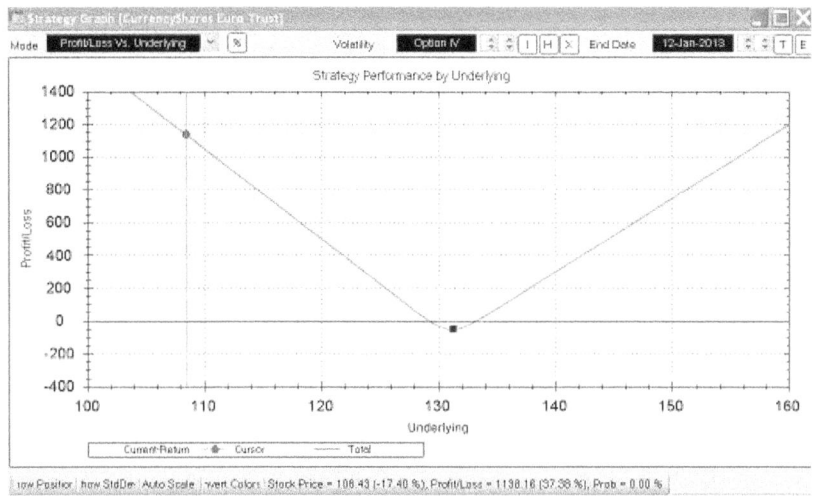

Criteria	Price	Change	Prob	Total	Total %	Total
Total Investment				3,044.58		
Total Debit				5,998.15		
Maximum Profit Poten...	Infinity	Infinity		Infinity		
Maximum Loss Risk	131.00	-0.21 %	46.71...	-108.15	+3.39 %	-4.61 %
Lower Breakeven	129.12	-1.63 %	25.41...	0.00		
Upper Breakeven	133.29	1.54 %	26.96...	0.00		
Total Theta [day]				-2.27	-0.07 %	

The spot / option trade requires more margin than an inverse option trade in the equities market. The maximum loss is much less because you are buying only one option. The delta of the option trade above was -.43 so I bought 43 shares of FXE to achieve delta neutral. This is my preferred trade in the OTC and futures market.

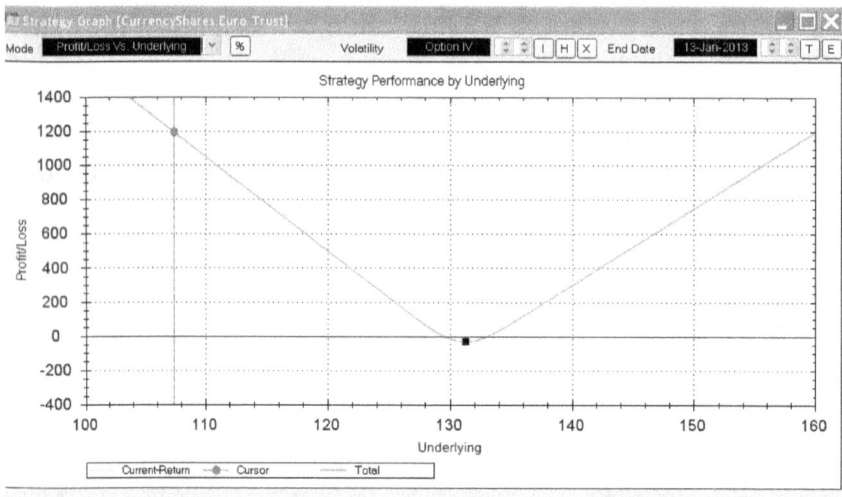

5 Volatility

Volatility can be the option traders best friend. Implied volatility can make or break your trade. Volatility alone can be traded and should be considered a major factor when placing an option trade.

Historical volatility is simply the range of price movement looking back in time.

	30 Day Av	30 Day Ma	100 Day A	100 Day Max
AUDCAD	12.86%	55.32%	13.10%	35.61%
AUDJPY	17.48%	100.81%	17.91%	67.21%
AUDUSD	14.96%	74.21%	15.27%	49.95%
EURAUD	12.83%	58.13%	13.05%	38.71%
EURCAD	12.15%	26.09%	12.23%	22.24%
EURCHF	5.16%	19.49%	5.31%	15.90%
EURGBP	9.21%	27.02%	9.24%	23.35%
EURJPY	13.46%	51.58%	13.59%	36.55%
EURUSD	12.09%	27.18%	12.14%	23.71%
GBPJPY	13.63%	55.64%	13.79%	41.50%
GBPUSD	10.60%	31.18%	10.69%	26.21%
USDJPY	11.94%	31.84%	12.05%	24.87%
USDCHF	13.03%	29.12%	13.08%	22.76%
USDCAD	9.99%	36.19%	10.09%	26.89%
GBPCHF	10.45%	35.84%	10.48%	28.12%

The chart above indicates that the historical volatility, or HV, of EURUSD is 12.14%. I use this number as an average volatility for the currency pair. Standard deviation is the formula used to calculate historic volatility. HV can be charted and it is useful to see if it is rising or falling.

Implied volatility is a forward looking estimate of future volatility. Implied volatility, or IV, is a major factor in option pricing. Low IV makes options cheap and high IV makes options expensive. Option traders buy low IV and sell high IV.

Implied Volatility Rates for Foreign Currency Options*
November 30, 2012

🖶 Printer version

	1WK	1MO	2MO	3MO	6MO	1YR	2YR	3YR
EUR	8.4	7.0	7.4	7.6	8.3	9.1	9.6	9.9
JPY	9.5	8.5	8.5	8.6	9.2	9.8	10.8	11.4
CHF	8.0	6.7	7.1	7.4	8.0	8.9	9.4	9.7
GBP	5.5	4.9	5.3	5.5	6.2	7.0	7.5	8.1
CAD	5.3	4.8	5.4	5.6	6.4	7.2	7.8	8.1
AUD	7.3	6.2	6.9	7.3	8.2	9.2	10.1	10.3
GBPEUR	5.8	5.0	5.3	5.5	6.0	6.8	7.3	7.8
EURJPY	10.9	10.4	10.5	10.7	11.2	12.0	13.0	13.6

Implied volatility rates for currencies are available from the Federal Reserve Bank of New York. These rates are published monthly and may have changed since published but its a good place to start your research. The chart above indicates if implied volatility is rising or falling.

By comparing the one week IV to the longer time frames we can determine whether IV is rising or falling. Implied volatility fluctuations are caused by economic and political events. Central bank activity can also create volatility swings.

Interest rate changes, employment reports, and other economic reports can also affect IV. These reports are normally scheduled and can be found on various economic calendars. ForexFactory.com provides economic calendars and publishes the results in a timely fashion.

Placing an option trade well in advance of a major announcement may provide an edge for the currency trader . Many spot traders develop systems based on trading the news. Increased volatility will increase the option value.

Fri Jan 4	2:00am	EUR		German Retail Sales m/m
	3:15am	EUR		Spanish Services PMI
	3:45am	EUR		Italian Services PMI
	4:00am	EUR		Final Services PMI
	4:30am	GBP		Services PMI
	4:30am	GBP		Net Lending to Individuals m/m
	4:30am	GBP		M4 Money Supply m/m
	4:30am	GBP		Mortgage Approvals
	5:00am	EUR		CPI Flash Estimate y/y
	5:00am	EUR		Italian Prelim CPI m/m
	8:30am	CAD		Employment Change
	8:30am	CAD		Unemployment Rate
	8:30am	CAD		RMPI m/m
	8:30am	CAD		IPPI m/m
	8:30am	USD		Non-Farm Employment Change
	8:30am	USD		Unemployment Rate
	8:30am	USD		Average Hourly Earnings m/m
	10:00am	USD		ISM Non-Manufacturing PMI
	10:00am	USD		Factory Orders m/m
	10:30am	USD		Natural Gas Storage
	11:00am	USD		Crude Oil Inventories
	3:30pm	USD		FOMC Member Yellen Speaks

This partial image of the ForexFactory website shows future announcements for various currencies. The USD non-farm employment change is a major report that could cause a rise in IV. The list is color coded to stress the importance or possible impact of the announcement. I refer to this service regularly.

I also refer to MarketWatch and CNBC for the current headlines that may affect currency volatility. When it comes to specific trade advise, I don't trust the news. Unreliable information can be leaked to create trader sentiment.

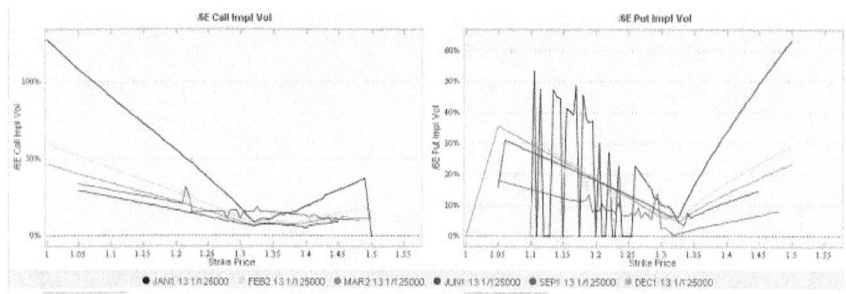

This implied volatility chart is from the Think or Swim trading platform available from TDAmeritrade. The chart illustrates that the ATM puts and calls on the Euro futures contract have the lowest IV and are therefore the least expensive. There is a wealth of information on this platform if you take the time to learn it.

The put / call ratio can be used as a market indicator of trader sentiment.

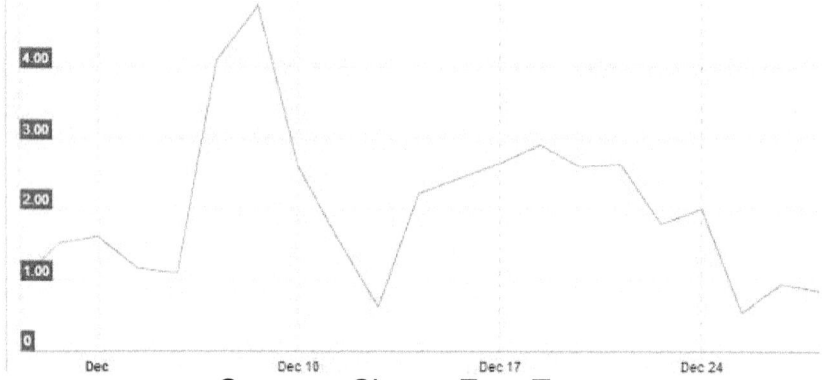

Currency Shares Euro Trust
Put / Call Ratio
AVAFIN.com

Many traders consider the put / call ratio to be a contrarian indicator. This axiom states that most traders will lose money and are on the wrong side of the trade. Depending on market conditions, I am normally in this camp. I think that most option traders are uninformed gamblers. In fact, I think that most forex traders in general are gambling for get rich quick profits. It is possible but not probable. A steady return on your investment should be the goal.

"Do it yourself" volatility studies are quick and easy on your favorite charting platform. I use the MT4 platform for forex and some futures and stocks.

The shaded areas illustrate option buying opportunities. Narrow Bollinger Bands equal low volatility. You can make a template of this study on the MT4 platform and apply it to your favorite currency pairs. Notice the price move after the period of low volatility. This is typical of all currencies.

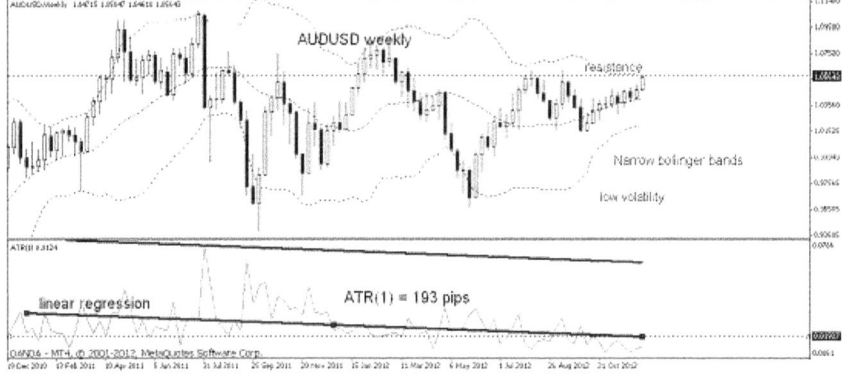

Linear regression is a handy tool that can be applied to indicators as well as price charts. This chart illustrates Average True Range narrowing. This currency pair is setting up for a directional move. I don't know which direction it is going but it doesn't matter if I'm making a non-directional trade. Since price is sitting on major resistance, my guess would be down.

Below is a volatility study created on the Think-or-Swim charting platform. The study shows decreasing volatility.

OptionsXpress provides an excellent charting platform with volatility studies and charts.

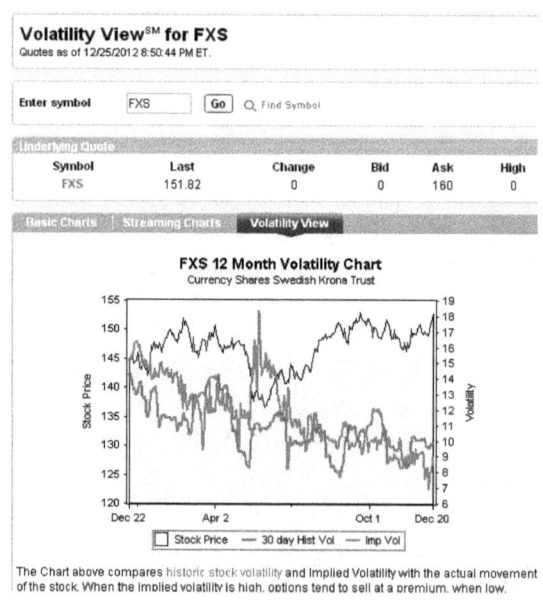

The Chart above compares historic stock volatility and Implied Volatility with the actual movement of the stock. When the Implied volatility is high, options tend to sell at a premium, when low.

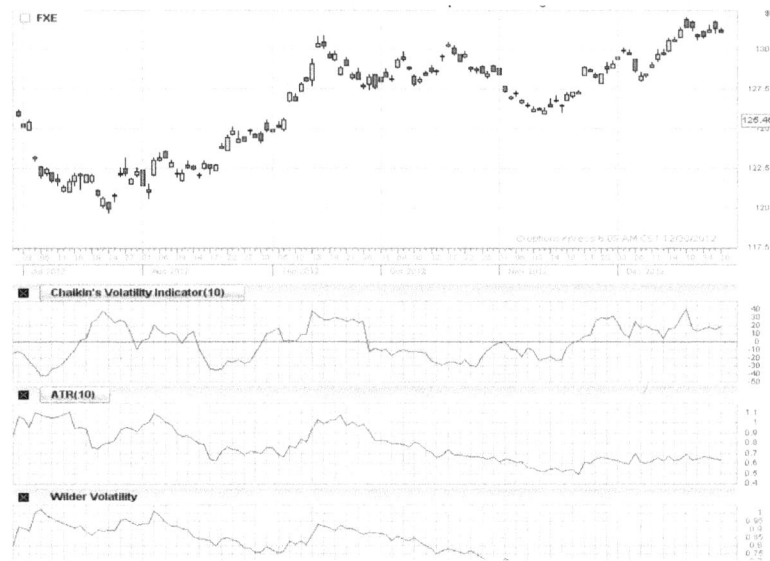

You can create your own custom application on their platform or use the predefined volatility study. In addition to these resources, TradingBlock.com offers option and volatility information including the current put / call ratio.

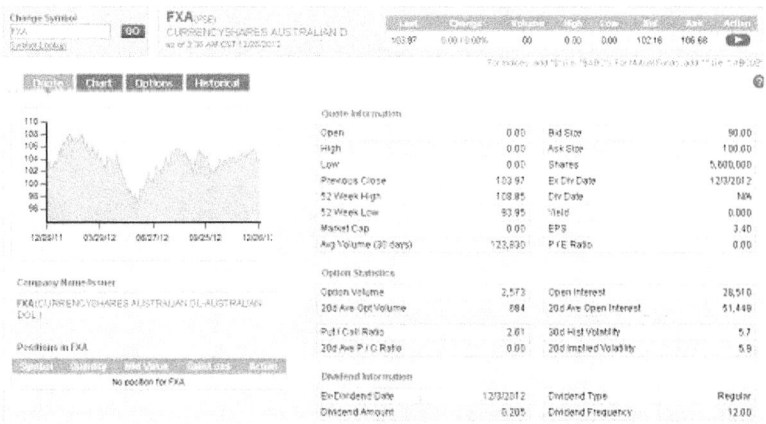

The effect of increased volatility can have a dramatic influence on your trade. An option trade can become profitable with little or no movement in the underlying price.

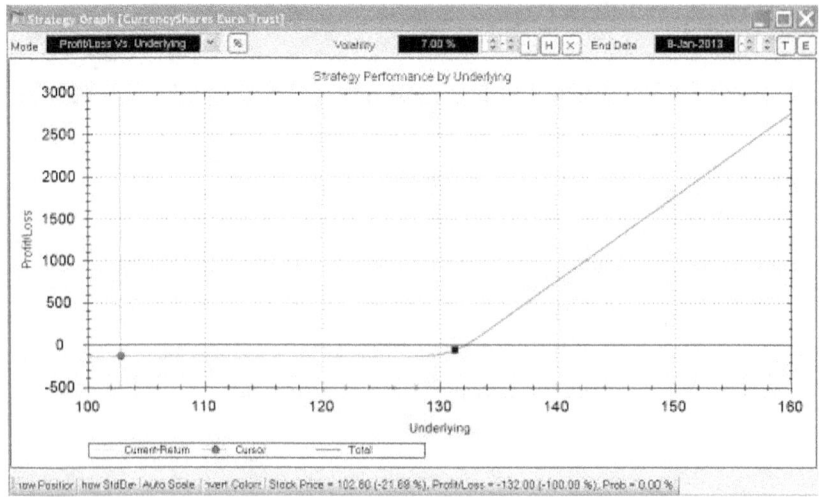

This graph is a long ATM call option on FXE. The implied volatility of this option is 7%. The graph below illustrates the effect of rising volatility on the option value.

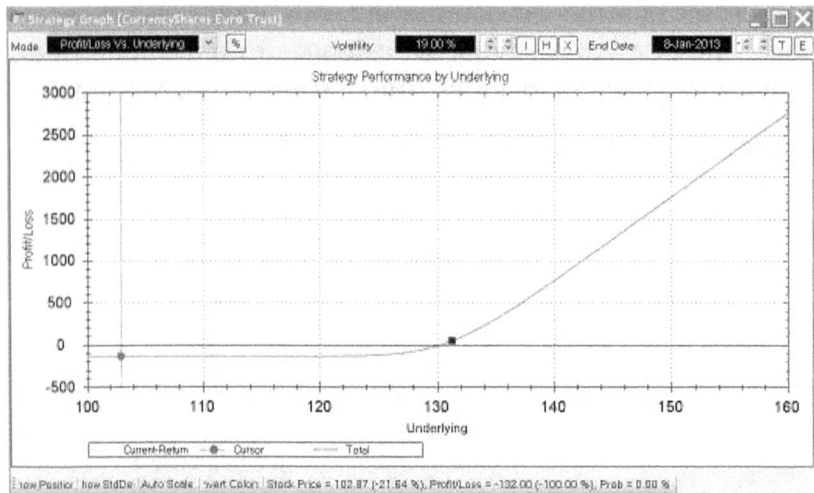

The black square on the chart is the current option value at price. This trade has become profitable with a rise in implied volatility to 19%. The price of the underlying asset has not moved at all. Buying low volatility gives the option trader an edge in the marketplace.

The same rules apply to inverse option trades. A rise in implied volatility can enhance your bottom line.

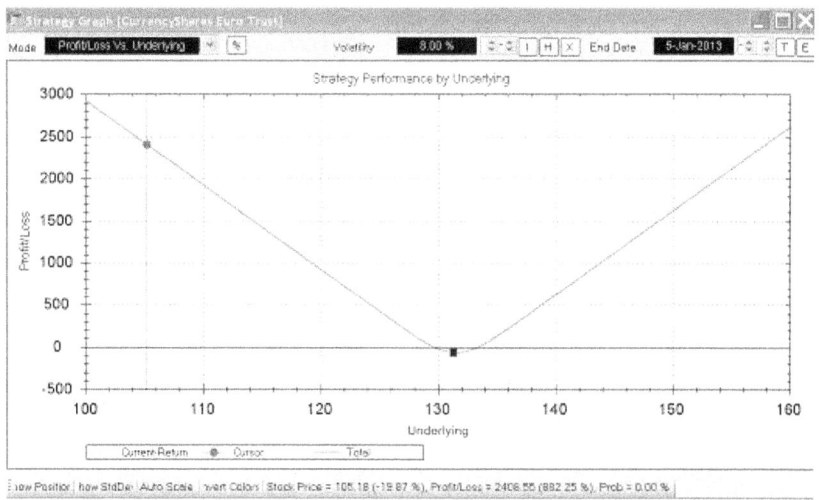

The graph above is an ATM call and put delta neutral trade on FXE. Implied volatility is 8%. The graph below illustrates a rise in IV to 12% with no movement in the underlying price.

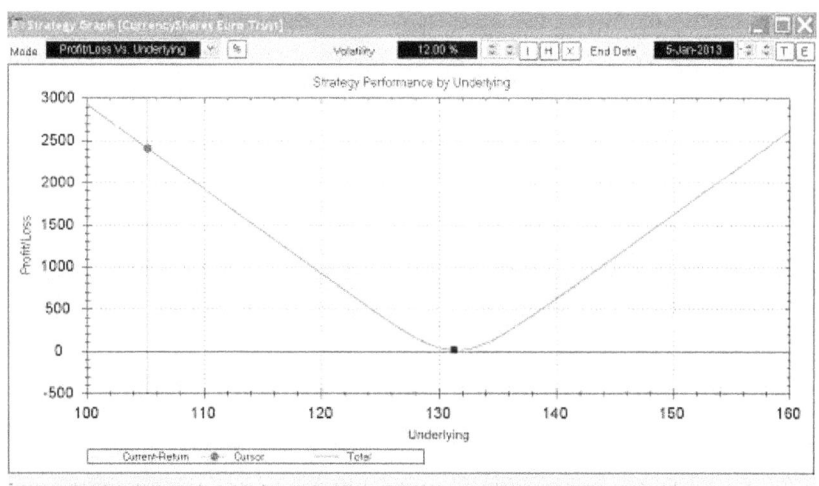

We need to have volatility on our side to overcome time erosion (theta), broker commissions, and the spread. These three factors eat away the profits.

6 Option Chains

Reading option chains may appear to be a complicated process but it is really quite simple. We want to know how much money we can make given a certain movement in the underlying price.

The fluctuation or volatility of currency prices provide the ideal playing field for option traders. There is a very high probability that the EURUSD currency pair will move at least 300 pips within a one month period.

I would venture to say that it would be nearly impossible for EURUSD or most any currency pair NOT to move 300 pips in any given month. That is not to say that it won't end up at the same price but it will fluctuate the 300 pips before so.

The option trader must decide when to exit the trade with a reasonable profit. Don't fall into the greed trap and don't cry about leaving money on the table. Take a reasonable profit and get out. If you can double your money on a trade, I would consider that an astounding profit.

A profit of 10% to 50% per month is an incredible return on your money. Approach the market like a banker rather than a gambler. Remember that 90% of all options expire worthless. That is because most option traders are indeed gamblers.

So here is fair warning. If you enter the market as a gambler, you will lose all of your money. The pro's are counting on it. Who do you think is selling the options? Selling (writing) options will not be the subject of this book.

Lets move on to reading option chains. View the option chain as a ladder. Climb up the ladder for a positive price move and climb down the ladder for a negative price move. I realize that this is opposite of what the strike prices are saying, but just do it.

This is how we can get an estimate of how much money we can make. This is not an exact science but an estimate of probable profitability of a trade. The following examples do not take into account THETA (time decay) or broker commissions.

Theta can be offset by buying low volatility. Of course, this is not always the case and having losing trades is a fact of life for all traders. But it will get the odds in our favor. The less amount of time we stay in the trade the less of a factor theta becomes.

If we did our spot trading homework, the trade will be entered at the appropriate time. You can refer to my first book, 2 Trade Smart, to learn the basic trading techniques. We need to put our full trading arsenal to work to get the odds in our favor. We want to exit any trade as quickly as possible with a reasonable profit.

As far as broker commissions are concerned, they can vary widely. Broker fees are less of a concern if you are trading 10 contracts or more. It is difficult to profit trading only one contract. On the other hand, market makers keep an eye on large traders and can widen the spread to confiscate your hard earned profits.

Trading option contracts with heavy volume and open interest will offset the market maker problem. Try to avoid thinly traded options, and there are plenty of them in the currency market. Heavily traded options also have better spreads.

The following graphic is an option chain of FXE. I am using FXE because it is the most heavily traded currency ETF in the equities market.

Last	Chg	Bid	Ask	Vol	OpInt	Action	▲ Strike ▼	Last	C
⊟	Jan13 Calls				(19 days to expiration)		XDE @ 132.2		
0	0	10.10	10.25	00	0	Trade | Detail ☐	122.00	0.30	
0	0	9.10	9.25	00	0	Trade | Detail ☐	123.00	0	
7.70	0	8.10	8.25	00	8	Trade | Detail ☐	124.00	0.66	
Your option contract will be worth $330.		5	7.25	00	IF the price of XDE moves up 300 pips	etail ☐	125.00	0.17	
		5	6.25	00		etail ☐	126.00	0.32	
		5	5.30	00		etail ☐	127.00	0.27	
0	0	4.28	4.35	00	0	Trade | Detail ☐	128.00	1.27	
1.45	0	3.30	3.40	00	2	Trade | De UP 300 pips	129.00	Current Price	
0.56	0	2.50	2.55	00	4	Trade | D UP 200 pips	130.00	of XDE 132.20	
1.62	0	1.76	1.79	00	125	Trade | C UP 100 pips	131.00	0.60	
1.25	0	1.14	1.17	00	147	Trade | Detail	132.00	0.93	
0.64	0	0.68	0.71	00	16	Trade | Detail ☐	133.00	1.28	
0.49	0	0.38	0.40	0	Buy a CALL $117 per contract	Trade | Detail ☐	134.00	0	
0	0	0.19	0.21	0				0	
0.15	0		0.11	00	READ the chain like a ladder. Just count the price movement up and down.			0	
If the price moves down 300 pips your option contract will be worth $19			0.06	00	0			0	
			0.04	00	0	This method will give us an approximate value		0	
			0.03	00	0			0	
0	0	0	0.10	00	0	Time decay and IV increase will affect the value		0	
0	0	0	0.10	00	0			0	

The strike prices are in increments of 100 pips. The equities market moves the decimal point two places to the left so that 132.00 means that the EURO is worth $1.32. To buy one share of FXE will cost you $132 plus commission. That is a spot trade, not an options trade.

Options contracts are per 100 shares. One ATM call option will cost you $117.00 USD. Walk up the chain for a positive price move. The value of this option will be approximately $330 USD if the spot price moves up 300 pips. We buy at the ASK and sell at the BID. The market maker keeps the difference.

Each strike price is equal to $1.00 in equities value or 100 pips in Forex value. You can research the spot movement of your equities asset on a forex chart. They are the same product reconfigured for the market. Equity products, futures products, and OTC products can all be charted on a forex platform.

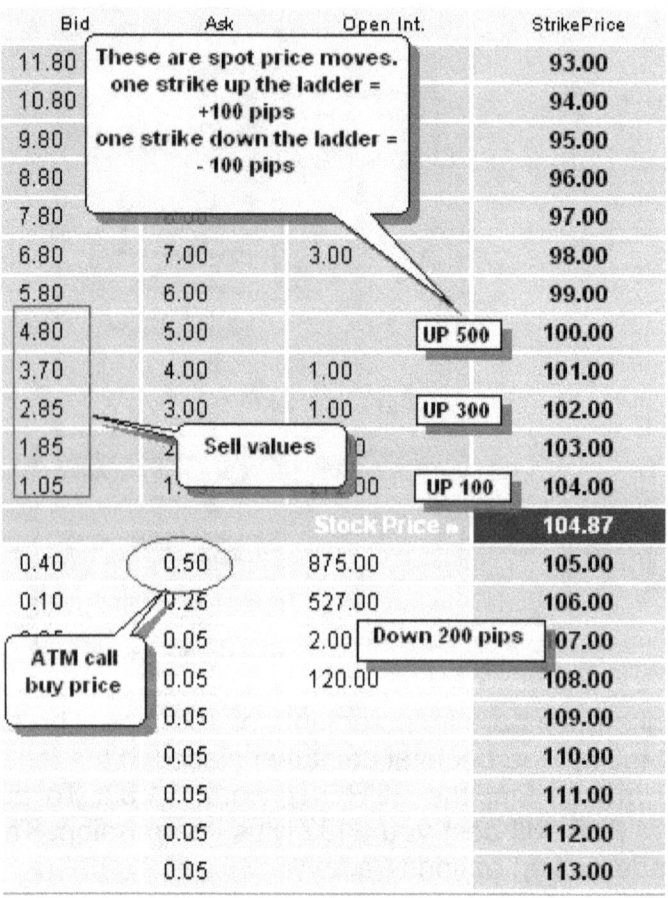

Bid	Ask	Open Int.	StrikePrice
11.80	These are spot price moves.		93.00
10.80	one strike up the ladder =		94.00
9.80	+100 pips		95.00
8.80	one strike down the ladder =		96.00
7.80	- 100 pips		97.00
6.80	7.00	3.00	98.00
5.80	6.00		99.00
4.80	5.00	UP 500	100.00
3.70	4.00	1.00	101.00
2.85	3.00	1.00 UP 300	102.00
1.85	Sell values	0	103.00
1.05	1	00 UP 100	104.00
		Stock Price	104.87
0.40	0.50	875.00	105.00
0.10	0.25	527.00	106.00
	0.05	2.00 Down 200 pips	07.00
ATM call buy price	0.05	120.00	08.00
	0.05		109.00
	0.05		110.00
	0.05		111.00
	0.05		112.00
	0.05		113.00

We climb up and down the ladder to estimate the possible outcome of a trade. The prices listed are current but may not reflect the actual future value. They are adequate for our purpose of trade feasibility. The trade may look good on paper but the actual results could be better or worse. That is the nature of the trading game.

CALLS						STRIKE			PUTS					
Quote	3.80	+0.80	BID	ASK	25	3,212	128.00	Quote	0.19	-0.0?	BID	ASK	14	4,?
Quote	2.50	+0.25	2.4?	2.5?	1	3,043	129.00	Quote	0.36	+0.03			28	9,?
Quote	1.77	-0.01	1.72	1.77	36	10,763	130.00	Quote	0.59	+0.07	0.59	0.61	18	9,?
Quote	1.16	-0.19	1.12	1.17	23	1,478	131.00	Quote	0.99	+0.10	0.99	1.02	337	3,?
Quote	0.70	-0.11	0.68	0.72	173	1,515	132.00	Quote	1.51	+0.14	1.54	1.56	42	3,?
Quote	0.39	-0.08	0.38	0.41	415	2,416	133.00	Quote	2.27	+0.19	2.23	2.27	2	5
Quote	0.22	+0.00	0.19	0.22	1	895	134.00	Quote	3.15	-0.60	3.00	3.10	2	3

The above example illustrates the bid / ask spread. If we buy one ATM put contract, it will cost us $156.00 USD. If the spot price of EURUSD (FXE) goes up 200 pips, the option contract will be worth approximately $59.00. If the spot price goes down 200 pips, the contract will be worth $300.00.

Can you see that by walking up and down the ladder we can easily see if our option trade can be profitable. We must consider the probability of price movement before option expiration. Will the underlying spot price move XX points within XX days. This can be forecasted through the use of technical analysis.

We will only allow options to expire worthless that are valued less than the brokers commission fee. We do not exercise options because we are not interested in assuming a spot position. We are simply buying and selling contracts for cash.

If you sell an equities option contract, the cash is immediately deposited into your account (unlike the sale of stock). The transaction is guaranteed by the Options Clearing Corporation, a quasi-government organization known as the OCC. Your broker must accept and pay you for the sale of your option.

If the option expires out of the money, the broker will not charge any fees. If the option expires in the money, your broker may or may not charge a fee. Read the agreement. We would prefer to sell our purchased option long before expiration because theta will eat away the profits. So we are looking for a sharp price move with a rise in volatility.

The following illustration will show you how to determine if an inverse option trade is feasible.

	BID	ASK		Strike	OPTION CHAIN FXE 50 pip increments				BID	ASK
10.00			630.00	126.00	quote 0.04	-0.01	22.00			
				126.50						
15.00	2.85	2.91	2,091	127.00	quote 0.06	-0.07	6.00	0.08	0.11
				127.50	quote				
52.00	1.97	2.02	3,212	128.00	quote 0.20	-0.10	542.00	0.19	0.22
				128.50	quote				
527.00	1.18	1.24	3,003	129.00	quote 0.43	-0.16	2,699	0.42	0.45
			5.00	129.50	quote				
			StockPrice	129.81					
159.00	0.62	0.66	10,758	130.00	Delta neutral inverse trade	-0.20	268.00	0.85	0.92
			11.00	130.50	BUY 2 call contracts				
84.00	0.26	0.30	1,427	131.00	BUY 2 put contracts	-0.27	1,102	1.48	1.52
				131.50	quote				
167.00	0.11	0.12	1,420	132.00	quote 2.30	-0.26	198.00	2.31	2.35
				132.50	quote				
60.00	0.03	0.05	2,189	133.00	quote 3.15	-0.30	13.00	3.25	3.35
				133.50	quote				
4.00	0.01	0.03	801.00	134.00	quote 3.15	-0.60	20.00	4.20	4.35

This is another option chain of FXE. We will make a delta neutral inverse option trade.

Buy 2 ATM call option contracts for $66x2= $122.00

Buy 2 ATM put option contracts for $92x2= $184.00

Delta +1 and delta -1 = zero or delta neutral

Total investment = $306.00

A 300 pip positive move results in:
The call options are worth $285 x 2 = $570
The put options are worthless.
The option value of $570 less the amount invested of $306 results in a gross profit of $264.00

A 300 pip negative move results in:
The put options are worth $325 x 2 = $650
The call options are worthless.
The option value of$650 less the amount invested of $306 results in a gross profit of $344.00

This trade can be profitable if EURUSD moves 300 pips or more before expiration. Theta and IV are not factored in.

Let's try a delta neutral inverse option trade on the Powershares QQQ Trust ETF.

378.00	4.01	4.07	21,807	63.00	quote	0.43	-0.01	553.00	0.42	0.46
52.00	3.18	3.24	5,479	64.00	quote	0.60		810.00	0.60	0.64
1,343	2.44	2.46	9,833	65.00	qu QQQ Trust ETF			1,105	0.85	0.89
7,602	1.73	1.76	9,674	66.00	qu		0.01	7,348	1.17	1.22
				66.63						
1,737	1.21	1.23	21,214	67.00	quote	1.58	0.04	1,935	1.62	1.66
1,093	0.75	0.77	55,939	68.00	quote	2.15	0.07	773.00	2.14	2.19
1,386	0.43	0.46	116,795	69.00	quote	2.87	0.15	198.00	2.85	2.92
545.00	0.24	0.25	42,212	70.00	quote	3.55	-0.09	789.00	3.60	3.72

Buy 2 ATM call option contracts for $123x2 = $246

Buy 2 ATM put option contracts fo $166x2 = $332

Delta+1 and delta -1 = zero or delta neutral

Total investment = $578

A $3 price increase results in:

The call options are worth $318x2 = $636

The put options are worth $60x2 = $120

The option values of $756 less the amount invested of $578 results in a gross profit of $178

A $3 price decrease results in:

The call options are worth $24x2 = $48

The put options are worth $360x2 = $720

The option values of $768 less the amount invested of $578 results in a gross profit of $190

This trade is not quite as good as the currency trade but still a workable trade. The QQQs are very heavily traded resulting in tight spreads.

Futures options chains are a bit different. The strike prices run in the opposite direction.

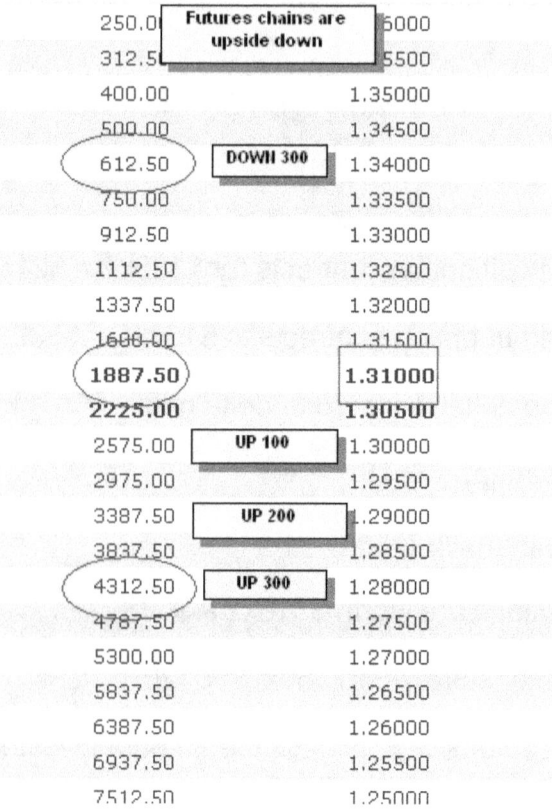

The commodity futures industry has their own way of doing things. We count down the ladder for a price increase and up the ladder for a price decrease. That's just the way it is. Barchart will post the actual premium. The premium must be multiplied by the contract value on most futures chains.

Futures chains are much longer than equity chains. Many professional traders sell (or write) far out of the money options. This practice could be considered risky but it is actually very lucrative.

Date	Strike	Symbol	Premium
2013-03-08		6E.H13.128000C	
2013-03-08	1.285	6E.H13.128500C	0.03070
2013-03-08	1.29	6E.H13.129000C	0.02710
2013-03-08	1.295	6E.H13.129500C	0.02380
2013-03-08	1.3	6E.H13.130000C	0.02060
2013-03-08	1.305	6E.H13.130500C	0.01780
2013-03-08	1.31	6E.H13.131000C	0.01510
2013-03-08	1.315	6E.H13.131500C	0.01280
2013-03-08	1.32	6E.H13.132000C	0.01070
2013-03-08	1.325	6E.H13.132500C	0.00890
2013-03-08	EURO FX Futures Chain	0C	0.00730

This is a partial view of a standard futures chain with the premium posted in the usual format. In the example above the ATM call premium is 0.01780. This number must be multiplied by the contract value of 125,000. The resulting price of the call option is $2,225.

Futures option contracts are based on the value of one full currency contract. In the case of Euro FX the contract size is $125,000 USD. This is the value of the underlying futures contract.

The underlying futures contract is a derivative contract with an expiration date. When trading options on futures you are in effect trading derivatives on derivatives. That's how crazy we have become but it sure is interesting.

Please, do not fall asleep and forget to exit your futures option trade. The underlying futures contract can be put to you at expiration. The futures contract can also be exercised at expiration and you could wake up with a boatload of Euro's. FX Options are available in American or European style.

You can sell your option anytime for a cash settlement, and that's what we do. Cash is king in our trading plan.

Current Prices | End-of-Day Prices | Options Quotes | Spread Quotes | Profile

» Latest Options   Daily Options ⓘ HELP   Options View: Merged » Split

Options Expiration:	03/08/13	Euro FX March 2013 Options
Days to Expiration:	63	Select Month: Mar 2013 ▾
Euro FX Mar 2013:	1.30800	
Price Value of Option Point: $125,000		Latest Options : 21:00 Friday, 4 January

Barchart.com offers free futures option chains. The image above shows the contract details such as the point value multiplier and days till expiration.

	CALLS	STRIKE	PUTS	
0.00400s				5112.50
0.004 *option prices X 125,000*	612.50	1.34000	0.03690s	4612.50
0.006	750.00	1.33500	*Futures options in 50 pip increments*	4125.00
0.00	912.50 *premium value*	1.33000		3662.50
0.00890s	1112.50	1.32500	0.02590s	3237.50
0.01070s	1337.50	1.32000	0.02270s	2837.50
0.01280s	1600.00	1.31500	0.01980s	2475.00
0.01510s	1887.50	1.31000	0.01710s	2137.50
0.01780s	2225.00	1.30500	0.01480s	1850.00
0.02060s	2575.00	1.30000	0.01260s	1575.00
0.02380s	2975.00	1.29500	0.01080s	1350.00
0.02710s	3387.50	1.29000	0.00910s	1137.50
0.03070s	3837.50	1.28500	0.00770s	962.50
0.03450s	4312.50	*Barchart calculates the premium for you*	0.00650s	812.50
0.03830s	4787.50		0.00540s	675.00

Barchart has been kind enough to multiply the premium for us. Futures option chains are in 50 pip increments which is an advantage for the trader. It gets our delta closer. The full chart includes volume and open interest. This page is too small to include the full chains.

After reading this book you should continue your education before trading options on futures. Futures have many advantages over equities but this publication is far to brief to fully explain option trading of any kind. My book is intended to open your eyes to the option trading possibilities and potential. Read the fine print before entering any contract.

CME Group offers the FX options brochure and a massive amount of educational services.

The CBOE and the OIC also offer an incredible amount of information and services.

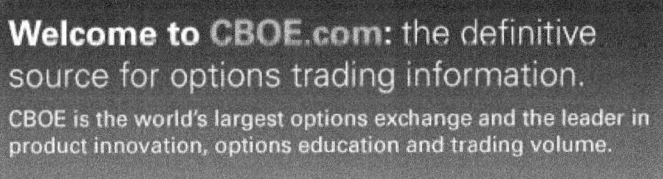

About The Options Industry Council

The Options Industry Council (OIC) was created to educate investors and their financial advisors about the benefits and risks of exchange-traded equity options. Options are a versatile but complex product, and that is why OIC conducts hundreds of seminars, distributes educational brochures, maintains a website, and offers live help from options professionals.

Futures option traders should subscribe to Ivolatility.com for a wealth of information including delta, theta, implied volatility and much more.

Expiry: 12/08/2006	Days: 14		Vola Skew								
Strike	Call/Put	Future Price	Settlement Price	Change (%)	Volume	OI	Implied Vola	Delta	Gamma	Theta	Alpha	Vega
⌁1.31	C	1.31	0.0084	0.01 (366.67 %)	1964	2363	8.03%	0.5109	19.4031	-0.0003	-66,566.2266	0.0010
	P	1.31	0.0080	-0.01 (-54.29 %)	0	69	8.02%	-0.4893	19.5221	-0.0003	-66,677.6250	0.0010
⌁1.32	C	1.31	0.0062	0.00 (416.67 %)	0	740	8.10%	0.4157	18.7930	-0.0003	-65,221.0352	0.0010
	P	1.31	0.0108	0.01 (0.00 %)	11	0	8.10%	-0.5847	18.8943	-0.0003	-65,373.2852	0.0010

I am not in favor of "too much information" because it ties up your brain and your time. But you should at least know which information you are overlooking.

You could analyze a trade to death and still end up with a loser. The most important elements are delta and implied volatility. You can not trade without this information. Delta and IV are located on the chain in the equities and OTC markets. I have not been able to locate it on a futures chain. A third party vendor is recommended.

This is a partial view of a futures options chain. All the futures FX contracts are heavily traded. I am using EuroFX.

0.00490s	612.50	1.34000	0.03690s	4612.50
0.00600s	750.00	1.33500	0.03300s	4125.00
0.00730s	912.50	1.33000	0.02930s	3662.50
0.00890s	1112.50	1.32500	0.02590s	3237.50
0.01070s	1337.50	1.32000	0.02270s	2837.50
0.01280s	1600.00	1.31500	0.01980s	2475.00
0.01510s	1887.50	1.31000	0.01710s	2137.50
0.01780s	2225.00	1.30500	0.01480s	1850.00
0.02060s	2575.00	1.30000	0.01260s	1575.00
0.02380s	2975.00	1.29500	0.01080s	1350.00
0.02710s	3387.50	1.29000	0.00910s	1137.50
0.03070s	3837.50	1.28500	0.00770s	962.50
0.03450s	4312.50	1.28000	0.00650s	812.50

Buy one ATM call for $1887

Buy one ATM put for $2137

Total Investment $4024

If spot has price increase of 300 pips:

The call value is $4312 and the put value is $812

Total value is $5124 less the $4024 investment

Gross profit = $1100

If spot has price decrease of 300 pips:

The call value is $612 and the put value is $4612

Total value is $5224 less the investment of $4024

Gross profit = $1200

This trade produces a better than 25% return on your investment in less than 4 weeks.

Time							Strike							Time
5:00:00 PM CT 1/8/2013	0	-	-	0.0307	-	-	12850	0.00	CME Group EUR USD Option Chain Multiplier 125,000			-	0.0083 b	0	1:55:06 AM CT 1/7/2013
1:09:52 AM CT 1/7/2013	0	-	-	0.0271	-	-	12900	0.00				-	0.0099 b	0	1:55:07 AM CT 1/7/2013
5:00:00 PM CT 1/8/2013	0	-	-	ATM CALL .8150 X 125,000 Premium = $1975	-	12950	0.011			0.0114 a	0.0117 b	0	1:55:07 AM CT 1/7/2013
1:56:01 AM CT 1/7/2013	0	0.0101 o	0.0185 a	0.0206	-0.05	0.0185 a	13000	0.0137 b	+0.0011	0.0126	0.0134 a	0.0137 o	0	1:55:01 AM CT 1/7/2013
1:56:01 AM CT 1/7/2013	0	0.0168 b	0.0158 a	0.0177	-0.0019	0.0158 a	13050	0.0160 b	+0.0013	0.0147	0.0156 a	0.0160 b	0	1:54:56 AM CT 1/7/2013
1:56:01 AM CT 1/7/2013	0	0.0138 b	0.0134 a	0.0151	-0.0017	0.0134 a	13100	0.0186 b	+0.0015	0.0171	0.0181 a	0.0186 b	0	1:55:01 AM CT 1/7/2013
1:56:07 AM CT 1/7/2013	0	0.0116 b	0.0112 a	0.0128	-0.0016	0.0112 a	13150	-	-	0.0199	-	-	0	5:00:00 PM CT 1/6/2013

This is the CME Group option chain for EUR/USD. The premium posted must be multiplied by the contract value. The EUR/USD contract value is 125,000 which is the same as the futures contract.

Reading the option chains can be as simple as climbing up and down the ladder. Trade analysis must provide a reasonable profit for the risk you are assuming. Be sure to allow enough time for the underlying asset to achieve the break even point.

Option premiums will be less expensive in the front expiry month. Inverse trades are best executed in the current month. These trades should be monitored and managed. If your analysis is wrong, the trade can be exited with an acceptable loss.

If you think the underlying spot will move dramatically in one direction you can exit one leg of the trade and let the other run. You can also double up and add a put or call to your position. The initial position can also be set up with a directional bias creating a positive or negative delta. The possibilities are endless using options.

FX FUTURES

FX futures and options on FX futures are available in a wide variety of products. CMEgroup offers full contract, mini-contract, and micro-contract futures. Options are available on the full contract scale but one delta .50 options contract can be offset with 5 e-micro contracts. There are a variety of possibilities for large and small traders.

Hedging FX futures Options with E-Micro contracts

Hedging futures FX options contracts with e-micro futures contracts can lead to innovative option strategies. Delta neutral and market neutral forex trading can be accomplished in an exchange traded arena. This type of inverse trading could only be done in the spot FX market prior to the introduction of the e-micro contracts.

There are a few points that are important to keep in mind when implementing a standard option hedge using e-micros. The e-micro in EUR/USD, GBP/USD and AUD/USD are exactly one tenth the standard contract, so it is a fairly straight forward calculation.

However, they are only approximately one tenth in USD/CAD, USD/CHF and USD/JPY as they are quoted in opposite terms and have a US$ notional ($10,000). Thus the calculation for determining the hedge ratio in these FX pairs will be:

(# option contract * option contract notional * option delta) / (e-micro $ notional * exchange rate in foreign currency per USD) = hedge ratio in # e-micro contracts

Formulating exact delta neutral trades is a professional tactic used by large traders. This is not necessary for small retail traders since most of our trades will be "approximately" delta neutral. But I will continue with the example in case you are interested.

Example:

Standard option in CAD/USD = C$100,000, assume option delta is 0.30 (30%)

E-micro USD/CAD notional = $10,000, assume the current exchange rate is 1.0410 (Standard contract would be ~0.9606) on the e-micro with equal maturity date of option's underlying.

Hedge ratio = (1 contract * C$100,000 * 0.30) / ($10,000 * C$/$ 1.0410) = 2.88, or just under 3 contracts. There will also be slight slippage in the hedge ratio from the changing exchange rate in addition to the changes coming from the option's delta. So exact delta neutral is elusive.

Keep in mind of the sign of the delta hedge. Normal rules will apply in the EUR/USD, GBP/USD and AUD/USD since they are quoted the same way. So if long a call option then sell the e-micro, if long a put option then buy the e-micro. BUT the rules are opposite with CAD/USD, JPY/USD and CHF/USD options. If you are long a CAD/USD Call, then BUY the USD/CAD e-micro. If you are long a CAD/USD Put, then SELL the USD/CAD e-micro. The new e-micro contracts are quoted in forex terms. Just make sure you are using the right contract.

E-micro Forex Futures Contract Specifications†

	Contract Size	Delivery	Minimum Tick Size	Contract Value	Ticker Symbols
E-MICRO EUR/USD FUTURES	12,500 euros	Physically Delivered	0.0001 USD/EUR (= US$1.25)	If USD/EUR = 1.3000 then contract = $16,250 (= €12,500 x $1.3000/€)	M6E
E-MICRO GBP/USD FUTURES	6,250 British pounds	Physically Delivered	0.0001 USD/GBP (= US$0.625)	If USD/GBP = 1.5000 then contract = $9,375 (= £6,250 x $1.5000/£)	M6B
E-MICRO AUD/USD FUTURES	10,000 Australian dollars	Physically Delivered	0.0001 USD/AUD (= US$1.00)	If USD/AUD = 0.6600 then contract = US$6,600 CAD (= 10,000 AUD x US$0.6600/USD)	M6A
E-MICRO USD/CAD FUTURES	10,000 U.S. dollars	Physically Delivered	0.0001 CAD/USD (= 1.00 CAD)	If CAD/USD = 1.2500 then contract = 12,500 CAD (= $10,000 x 1.2500 CAD/USD)	M6C
E-MICRO CAD/USD FUTURES	10,000 CAD	Physically Delivered	0.0001 USD/CAD (= US$1.00)	If USD/CAD = 0.9524 then contract = $9,524 (= 10,000 CAD x $0.9524/CAD)	MCD
E-MICRO USD/CHF FUTURES	10,000 U.S. dollars	Physically Delivered	0.0001 CHF/USD (= 1.00 CHF)	If CHF/USD = 1.2000 then contract = 12,000 CHF (= $10,000 x 1.2000 CHF/$)	M6S
E-MICRO CHF/USD FUTURES	12,500 CHF	Physically Delivered	0.0001 USD/CHF (= US$1.25)	If USD/CHF = 1.0256 then contract = $12,820 (= 12,500 CHF x $1.0256/CHF)	MSF
E-MICRO USD/JPY FUTURES	10,000 U.S. dollars	Physically Delivered	0.01 JPY/USD (= ¥100)	If JPY/USD = 93.00 then contract = ¥930,000 (= $10,000 x 93.00¥/$)	M6J
E-MICRO JPY/USD FUTURES	1,250,000 JPY	Physically Delivered	0.000001 USD/JPY (= US$1.25)	If USD/JPY = 0.011765 then contract = $14,706 (= ¥1,250,000 x $0.011765/¥)	MJY
E-MICRO USD/RMB (CNY) FUTURES	10,000 USD (≈ RMB 64,830)	NDF-Style Cash-Settled	0.0010 RMB/USD (= 10 RMB)	If RMB/USD = 6.3805 then contract = 63,805 RMB (= $10,000 x 6.3805 RMB/$)	MNY

If you are creating an inverse spot/option trade, be sure to use the correct format. For example, if you purchase a CHF/USD futures option, hedge it with the CHF/USD e-micro contract.

As a general example:

1 futures contract on the Swiss Franc is worth $125,000

2 ATM delta .50 options on this contract is worth $125,000

10 e-micro CHF/USD futures contracts are worth $125,000

Current Prices | End-of-

» **Latest Options**   Daily Options   @ HEL

Options Expiration:	03/08/13
Days to Expiration:	60
Swiss Franc Mar 2013:	1.08540
Price Value of Option Point:	$125,000

The price value of the option point is the same as the contract value. The e-micro contract is one tenth the size. This could enable you to hedge one delta .40 option with four e-micro contracts. A delta .30 option would require three e-micro contracts.

All futures volume reports are delayed by one day. So the volume you are seeing is from yesterday. Some brokers may estimate the volume but the numbers are not actual current volume.

The closest actual volume we can get on spot forex is the tick volume. It is available on the MT4 forex platform. Practice accounts are free, therefore forex analysis is free. There is not much related to futures that is free.

A tick is one single price movement. Ticks per time period result in a quantifiable or measurable volume estimate. In my opinion it is an accurate estimate of actual dollar volume.

Futures trading requires a little extra effort but they are working on simplification. Trading standardized and regulated contracts is safer than trading over the counter. But for speed and simplicity OTC wins hands down. The US forex brokers are regulated by the CFTC and they trade OTC. Over the counter options are not available to US traders. I keep looking.

CME FX options expiration procedure

CME FX options on the six major currencies are AUTO-EXERCISED against a daily fixing with no choice to the holder (buyer) of the option. The daily fixing is computed by CME Group and is based on a 30 second volume weighted average price of trades in the underlying futures occurring on CME Globex immediately preceding the 9:00 a.m. expiry (for European-style) and 2:00 p.m. expiry (for American-style). This daily fixing is published in real time on the CME Group website at:

cmegroup.com/fxfixing-price.

All in-the-money (ITM) options (1 pip or more) will be exercised and all at-the-money (ATM) and out-of-the-money (OTM) options will be abandoned with no recourse.

Be careful to close out your trades if they are in the money. Let the OTM options expire worthless to save you the commission fee. The above notice should serve as fair warning.

Trading futures and options on futures requires more education than trading equities, spot, or OTC options. Before entering this market, take the time to learn the basics. You can get into trouble if you don't know what you are doing. So keep your trigger finger off the button until you fully understand the implications.

Some broker platforms are the same way. The OptionsXpress platform is designed for retail traders and is very forgiving. The Interactive Brokers trading platform is unforgiving and requires a learning curve. If you press the wrong button, too bad, you are screwed. But you can't beat the broker fees.

Currency option open interest can be found on the CME website. They provide a tool that shows changes in open interest.

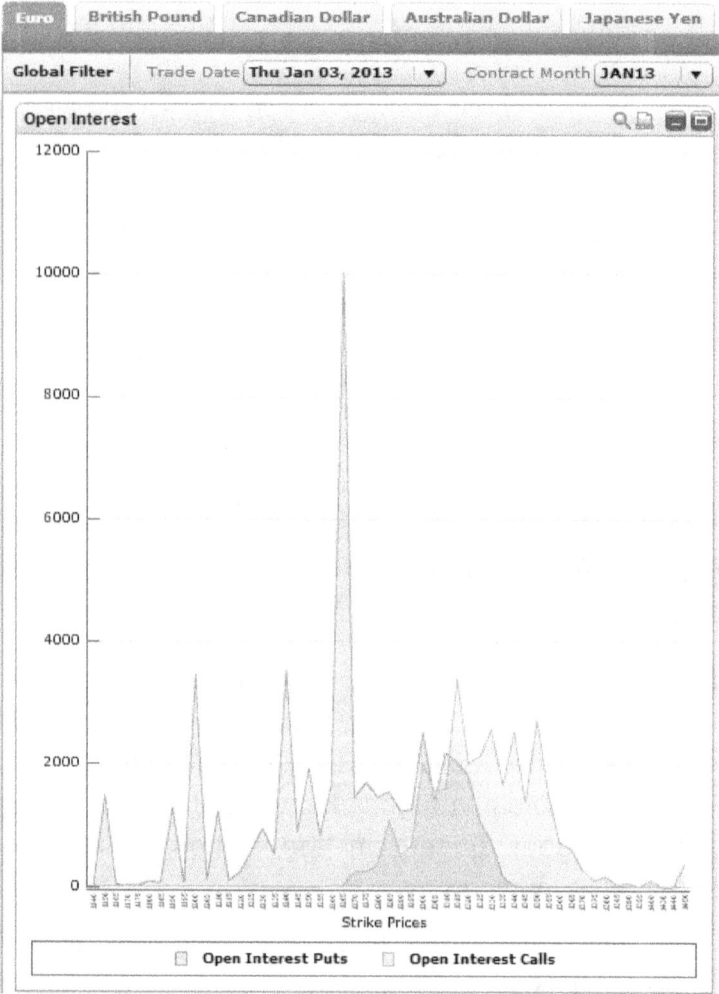

If you run your cursor over the chart it will provide the strike price and open interest. The large spike above is a trader selling way out of the money options. The price chart below will show you where the strike price is.

EUR/USD

The lower doted line is the strike price the chart indicated

13 Nov 2012 22 Nov 2012 2 Dec 2012 11 Dec 2012 20 Dec 2012 31 Dec 2012

This is a daily chart of EURUSD. The puts were sold at the lower dotted line because the price will never make it there before expiration and the seller will pocket the premiums. Selling a put gives you the obligation to buy the asset at the strike price selected.

Remember that all the available tools and services in the currency markets are inter-related and can be used to analyze a trade. You can use futures information to analyze an equities trade or a spot trade.

If your pockets are deep enough, you can hedge a spot/options inverse trade in separate accounts. The spot trade could be with a forex broker and the options leg with a futures or equities broker. The only problem is that one of these accounts will lose money while the other account profits by a greater amount.

I am a visual trader. I like to perform my analysis using charts and graphs. The Think-or-Swim program offers a number of visual aids. It is free to use with a TDAmeritrade account.

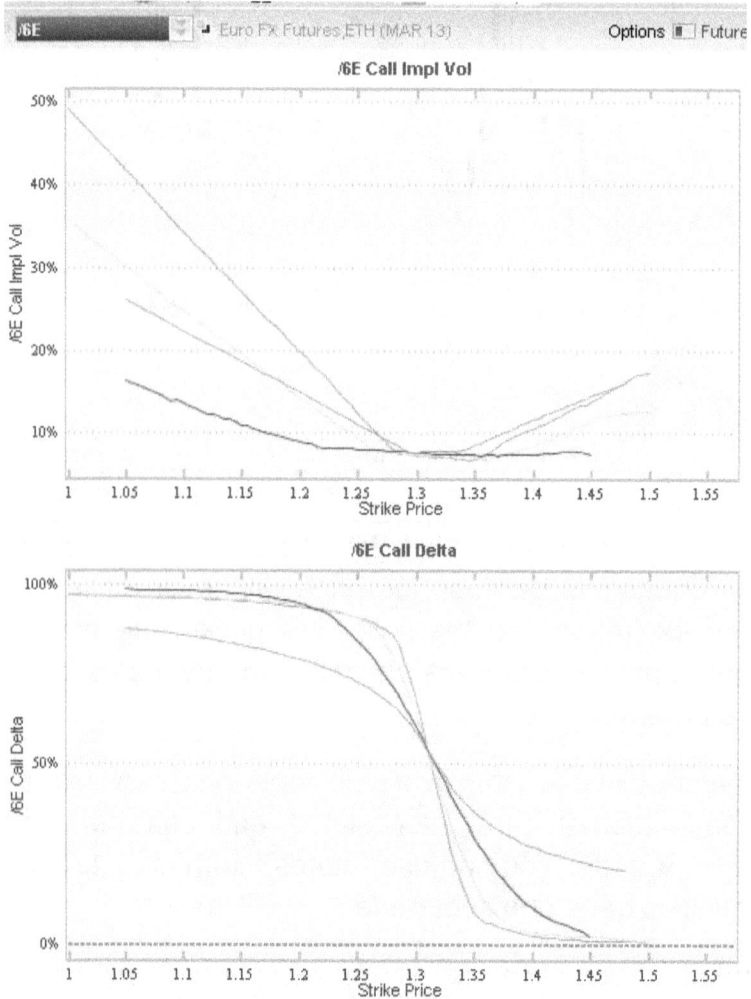

These graphs are Implied Volatility and option delta of the Euro FX options. Notice that the lowest IV and delta .50 are ATM options closest to the spot price. The inverse trades work best using ATM options.

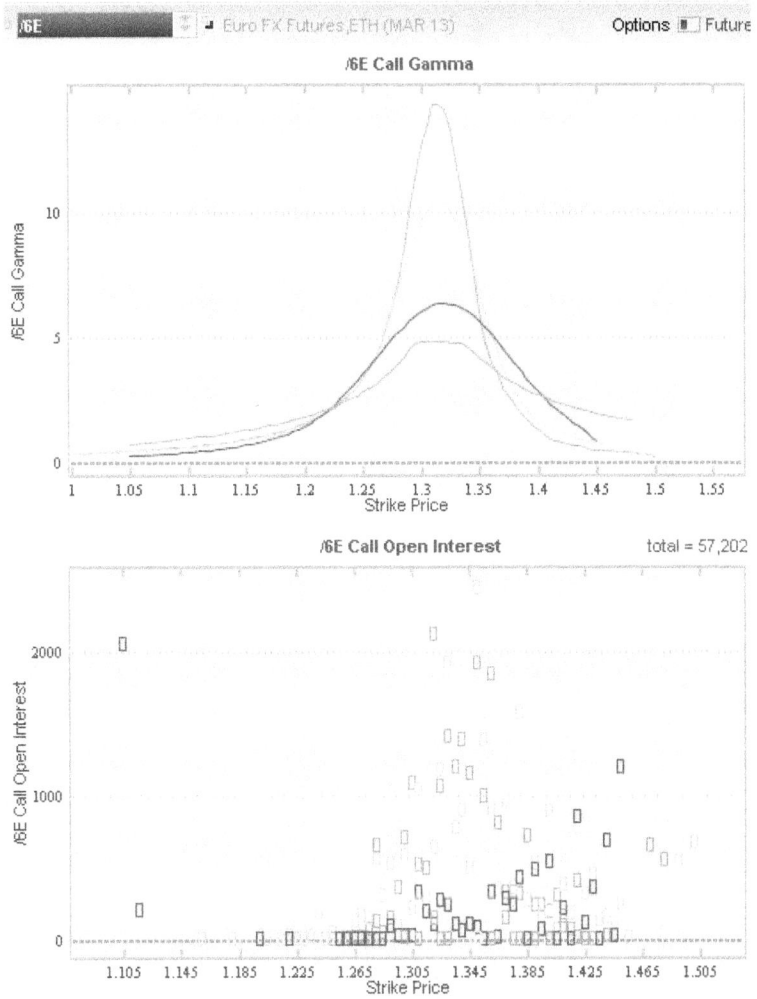

This chart shows gamma and open interest for calls and puts. Gamma is greatest at the money and gamma is our best friend. The way out of the money puts are the little squares on the left of the lower chart. The large spike on the previous chart reflects these sold puts. The Think-or-Swim application is very useful. Open a small account and it's free to use for your analysis.

8 OTC OPTIONS

The currency OTC options market is not available to US retail traders. Too bad for me and other US residents. This chapter is dedicated to the rest of the world.

OTC or over the counter options trade the same as exchange traded options except there is no exchange. Foreign Exchange trading is the largest market in the world and is traded by businesses and institutions in every country. It is too large to have a central exchange.

The world bankers have set up an unregulated over the counter trading arena. Traders exchange currencies on the open market. Buyers and sellers agree on terms and place trades on platforms controlled by large banks.

Exchange traded options in the US are regulated, standardized, and payment is guaranteed by the OCC. The OTC option market requires a counter-party to your trade. You can buy an option if someone is selling an option but you can't sell your option unless someone wants to buy it.

This could result in a total loss for the trader on the wrong side of a trade. But the market is extremely liquid and you would have to venture far off the beaten path to encounter such a problem. Trading ATM options on major pairs should present no such liquidity problem.

OTC trading platforms are very fast and extremely easy to use. You can make or lose money quickly. One big advantage is that you can trade spot and options on the same platform.

If you are creating an inverse spot / option trade the margin needed will be very small because you are entering opposite positions.

The platforms are well suited for day trading options. They are fast and easy to navigate. IV and delta information is right in front of your face. You can buy or sell in seconds. It is almost as if these guys know what they are doing.

EUR/USD Jan 13 Call

Parity		Expiration		Type			Bid	1.30359	Ask	1.30379
EUR/USD		January 2013		Call		Request	High	1.30796	Low	1.30276
							Exp. Date (FST)		01/17/2013 16:00	

Option	Bid	Ask	High	Low	Volatility	Delta
EUR/USD Jan 17 4PM 1.2701 Call	0.0332	0.0342	0.0379	0.0329	0.0759	0.9786
EUR/USD Jan 17 4PM 1.2751 Call	0.0284	0.0294	0.0330	0.0280	0.0753	0.9585
EUR/USD Jan 17 4PM 1.2801 Call	0.0237	0.0247	0.0282	0.0233	0.0747	0.9250
EUR/USD Jan 17 4PM 1.2851 Call	0.0191	0.0201	0.0235	0.0188	0.0742	0.8731
EUR/USD Jan 17 4PM 1.2901 Call	0.0149	0.0159	0.0190	0.0147	0.0736	0.7995
EUR/USD Jan 17 4PM 1.2951 Call	0.0111	0.0121	0.0148	0.0110	0.0730	0.7035
EUR/USD Jan 17 4PM 1.3001 Call	0.0078	0.0088	0.0111	0.0078	0.0724	0.5892
EUR/USD Jan 17 4PM 1.3051 Call	0.0052	0.0062	0.0079	0.0052	0.0724	0.4655
EUR/USD Jan 17 4PM 1.3101 Call	0.0032	0.0042	0.0054	0.0032	0.0724	0.3455
EUR/USD Jan 17 4PM 1.3151 Call	0.0017	0.0027	0.0034	0.0017	0.0723	0.2396
EUR/USD Jan 17 4PM 1.3201 Call	0.0008	0.0018	0.0021	0.0008	0.0723	0.1546
EUR/USD Jan 17 4PM 1.3251 Call	0.0002	0.0012	0.0012	0.0002	0.0723	0.0926
EUR/USD Jan 17 4PM 1.3301 Call	0.0000	0.0010	0.0006	0.0000	0.0722	0.0513
EUR/USD Jan 17 4PM 1.3351 Call	0.0000	0.0010	0.0003	0.0000	0.0722	0.0263
EUR/USD Jan 17 4PM 1.3401 Call	0.0000	0.0010	0.0001	0.0000	0.0721	0.0124

Option volatility and delta are right on the option chain on this IKON Prodigy platform screen shot. You can select parity, in this case EUR/USD, expiration date, and puts or calls. Contract size on this particular platform is 10,000. An option value of 0.0149 would be $149.00.

Depending on the broker and type of account opened, the trade size will normally be one full contract(100,000) or one mini contract (10,000). One full contract is approximately equal to a spot trade for $10 per pip. One mini contract would be equal to trading spot for $1 per pip.

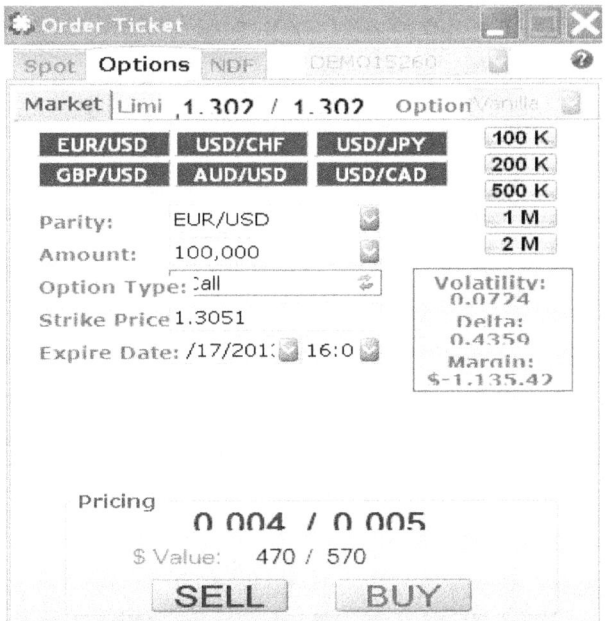

This is the Ikon order ticket with all the important information at hand. Volatility, delta, margin, spread, strike and everything you need to know. Below is the spot ticket.

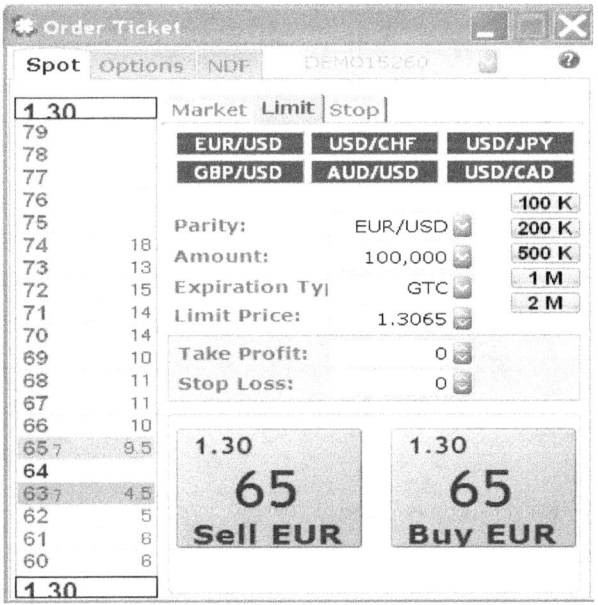

Fx Bridge technologies has developed a platform that is easy to use and very intuitive.

EUR/USD		13 DAYS TO EXPIRY 18-Jan-13 23:59 GMT		
Sell 1.30 **67**₀	3.0		Buy 1.30 **70**₀	
puts		strike	calls	
Bid	Ask		Bid	Ask
.00389	.00459	**1.28500**	.02562	.02632
.00521	.00591	**1.29000**	.02194	.02264
.00682	.00752	**1.29500**	.01854	.01924
.00872	.00942	**1.30000**	.01545	.01615
.01095	.01165	**1.30500**	.01267	.01337
.01354	.01424	**1.31000**	.01027	.01097
.01648	.01718	**1.31500**	.00820	.00890
.01972	.02042	**1.32000**	.00644	.00714
.02325	.02395	**1.32500**	.00498	.00568
.02704	.02774	**1.33000**	.00377	.00447

You can scroll up and down the option chain and click on bid or ask to sell or buy an option. Puts are on the left and calls are on the right. If you mouse over an option premium the IV and delta will be displayed.

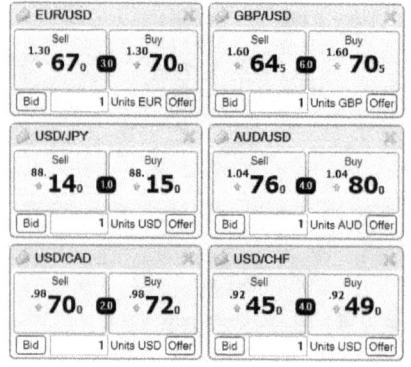

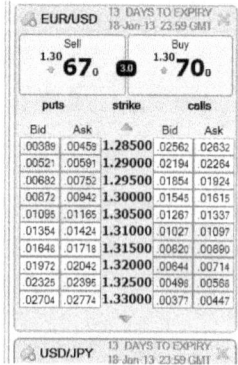

Spot and options order tickets can be displayed side by side.

All of the OTC platforms offer a free practice account. Get to know your platform before trading with real money.

Saxo Bank is located in Denmark and has many offices located in Europe and the far east. They are a very large OTC option dealer. The platform is retail trader friendly.

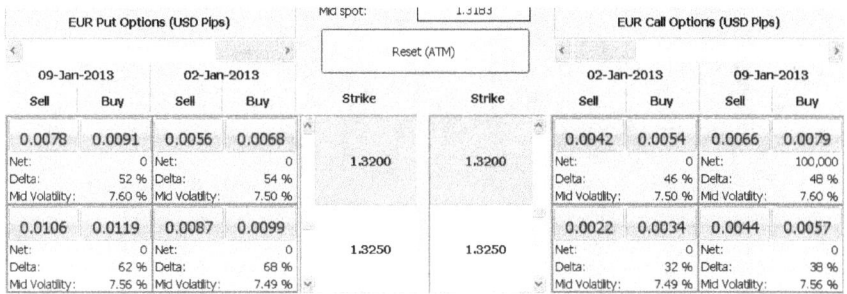

EUR Put Options (USD Pips)				Mid spot: 1.3183		EUR Call Options (USD Pips)			
09-Jan-2013		02-Jan-2013		Reset (ATM)		02-Jan-2013		09-Jan-2013	
Sell	Buy	Sell	Buy	Strike	Strike	Sell	Buy	Sell	Buy
0.0078	0.0091	0.0056	0.0068	1.3200	1.3200	0.0042	0.0054	0.0066	0.0079
Net: 0		Net: 0				Net: 0		Net: 100,000	
Delta: 52 %		Delta: 54 %				Delta: 46 %		Delta: 48 %	
Mid Volatility: 7.60 %		Mid Volatility: 7.50 %				Mid Volatility: 7.50 %		Mid Volatility: 7.60 %	
0.0106	0.0119	0.0087	0.0099	1.3250	1.3250	0.0022	0.0034	0.0044	0.0057
Net: 0		Net: 0				Net: 0		Net: 0	
Delta: 62 %		Delta: 68 %				Delta: 32 %		Delta: 38 %	
Mid Volatility: 7.56 %		Mid Volatility: 7.49 %				Mid Volatility: 7.49 %		Mid Volatility: 7.56 %	

The Saxo option chain is a bit awkward in my opinion because there is not enough strikes showing but I can make it work. You scroll up and down the chain for the various strike prices.

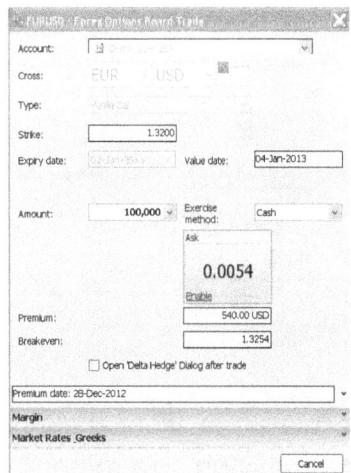

The order ticket is simple and to the point. Notice the check box "open delta hedge" at bottom of ticket. Margin and greeks are on a drop down menu.

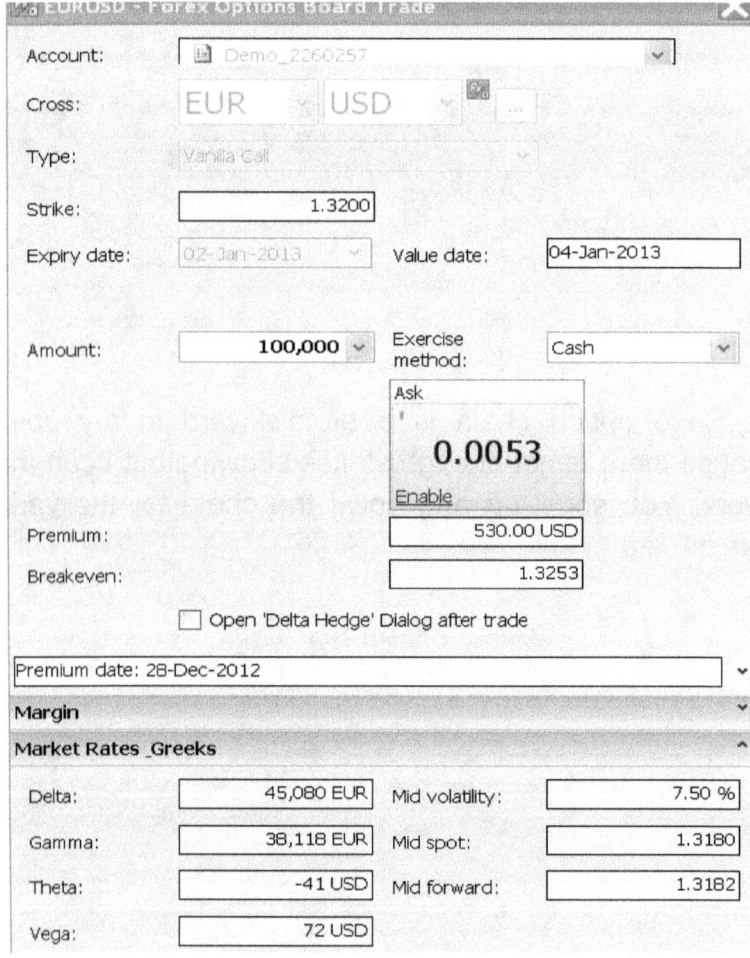

All the information we need is at the bottom of the ticket. Delta is given in spot position size rather than a percentage.

The program figures out an exact delta hedge for you.

The spot / option inverse trade is just a click away. Click on enable to receive a current price and then click hedge position.

The hedge confirmation will pop up immediately. It don't get any easier than this. The entire trade takes less than a minute. Try that on an equities platform.

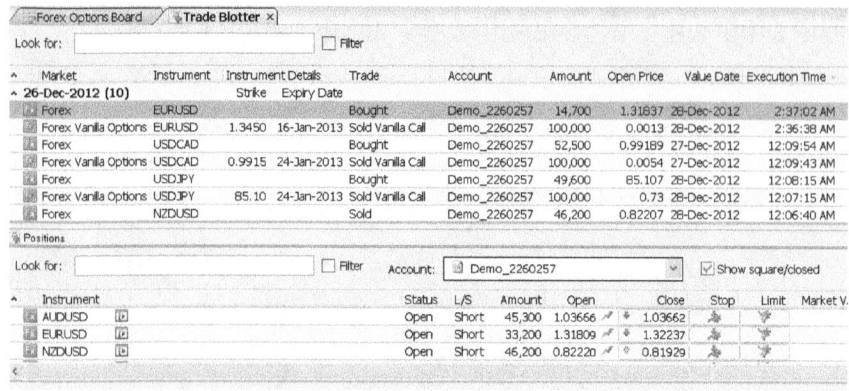

The trade blotter shows your account activity at a glance. Open and closed positions, available margin, and everything you need to know. They almost make it too easy to trade.

OTC options are my trading method of choice, unfortunately I can not trade them in the USA. The platform is so easy to use that it may entice you to over-trade. Trading without thinking is a bad thing. Take the time to carefully plan your trades just like you were trading on a futures platform.

Fools rush in. The OTC platform makes it too easy to jump on a trade. Your trade should be planned before opening the trading platform. Don't think with your index finger.

9 FX EQUITIES

Trading options on currency ETFs is not my first choice but it is a good place to start, especially for novice option traders. Stick to the most heavily traded currency shares.

currencySHARES® SNAPSHOT	Flag	Symbol
CurrencyShares Australian Dollar Trust		FXA
CurrencyShares British Pound Sterling Trust		FXB
CurrencyShares Canadian Dollar Trust		FXC
CurrencyShares Chinese Renminbi Trust		FXCH
CurrencyShares Euro Trust		FXE
CurrencyShares Japanese Yen Trust		FXY
CurrencyShares Swedish Krona Trust		FXS
CurrencyShares Swiss Franc Trust		FXF

Spot trading these assets is very expensive so just trade the options. Spot trading is best and much less expensive with a forex broker. If you are going to trade these options you should have a forex account to research the charts. All the forex brokers offer practice accounts and live accounts can be opened with very small deposits.

Just about all the stock brokers carry options and some specialize in options. Those that specialize in options will be able to provide more options tools and information. Volatility studies and option greeks are not negotiable, you must have them to trade profitably.

If you are a novice to options, I would suggest OptionsXpress. They offer all the option tools, chains, graphs, and charts. One very important factor for option traders is fair value. Fair value is the theoretical value of the option determined by the pricing formula being used. The fair value will tell you if the option is over-priced or under-priced.

Since we are buying options, we are looking for under-priced options, or at least fairly priced options. There are a number of calculators on the web to figure this stuff out but that sounds like a chore to me. OptionsXpress provides the option pricer that does all the work for you.

▲ Strike ▼	Last	Bid	Ask	Theo Value
February 2013				
112.00	0	17.80	17.90	17.963
113.00	0	16.80	16.90	16.964
114.00	0	15.80	15.90	15.966
115.00	0	14.80	14.90	14.967
116.00	0	13.80	13.90	13.968
117.00	0	12.80	12.90	12.969
118.00	0	11.80	11.90	11.970
119.00	0	10.80	10.90	10.971
120.00	0	9.80	9.90	9.972
121.00	0	8.80	8.90	8.973
122.00	0	7.80	7.90	7.976
123.00	0	6.80	6.90	6.982
124.00	0	5.80	5.90	5.999
125.00	5.28	4.85	4.95	5.037
126.00	5.15	3.95	4.05	4.104
127.00	4.40	3.05	3.15	3.230
128.00	2.29	2.30	2.35	2.455
129.00	1.88	1.61	1.66	1.777
130.00	1.00	1.06	1.10	1.203
131.00	0.67	0.65	0.68	0.779
132.00	0.39	0.38	0.40	0.482
133.00	0.20	0.20	0.22	0.269

The preceding chart is fair value for calls. It shows the bid, ask, and theoretical value of each call at each strike price. The shaded shaded area are the ATM calls. The ATM calls are under-priced, and therefore a bargain. The next image is for puts.

▲ Strike ▼	Last	Bid	Ask	Theo Value
February 2013				
112.00	0	0	0.03	0.000
113.00	0	0	0.03	0.000
114.00	0	0	0.03	0.000
115.00	0	0	0.03	0.000
116.00	0	0	0.03	0.000
117.00	0	0	0.03	0.000
118.00	0	0	0.03	0.000
119.00	0	0	0.03	0.000
120.00	0	0	0.04	0.000
121.00	0.04	0	0.04	0.001
122.00	0	0.01	0.04	0.002
123.00	0.00	0.03	0.05	0.000
124.00	0.13	0.05	0.08	0.024
125.00	0.12	0.11	0.13	0.060
126.00	0.27	0.19	0.21	0.127
127.00	0.33	0.33	0.35	0.252
128.00	0.60	0.54	0.57	0.478
129.00	0.88	0.86	0.89	0.802
130.00	1.34	1.31	1.35	1.234
131.00	1.95	1.89	1.94	1.813
132.00	2.64	2.65	2.66	2.524
133.00	3.76	3.40	3.50	3.325
134.00	4.40	4.30	4.40	4.206

The ATM puts are slightly over-priced. This may indicate the option markets expectation of a decline in spot price. The puts are not far enough out of line that it would influence my trade.

There are many types of option strategies and volumes of books and websites devoted to these strategies. Occasionally, I will trade a credit spread or a calendar spread. There are many variations and you can invent a few of your own. Get the free Options Oracle program from Samoa Sky and experiment with these strategies. Most of the popular strategies are automated within the program.

After learning about the non-linear nature of the option trade, you will better understand why these strategies work. The purpose of this book is to explain the basic nature of option trading. The possibilities are unlimited using options. I wish you the best in your option trading.

To learn basic spot trading techniques order my book from Amazon.com

2 Trade*Smart   High Probability, Low Risk Trades

www.ingramcontent.com/pod-product-compliance
Lightning Source LLC
Chambersburg PA
CBHW071247170526
45165CB00003B/1272